1000 THINGS YOU SHOULD KNOW ABOUT

MYTHS & LEGENDS

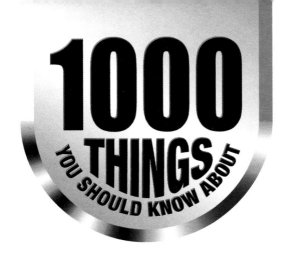

1000 THINGS YOU SHOULD KNOW ABOUT

MYTHS & LEGENDS

Vic Parker

Miles Kelly
PUBLISHING

First published in 2004 by
Miles Kelly Publishing Ltd
Bardfield Centre, Great Bardfield
Essex, CM7 4SL

Copyright © 2004 Miles Kelly Publishing Ltd

2 4 6 8 10 9 7 5 3 1

Editor: Kate Miles
Art Director: Debbie Meekcoms
Design: DPI Colour Digital Ltd
Picture Research: Liberty Newton
Production: Estela Boulton

British Library Cataloguing-in-Publication Data
A catalogue record for this book is available from the British Library

ISBN 1-84236-439-1

Printed in China Hong Kong Singapore Thailand
info@mileskelly.net
visit us at our website: www.mileskelly.net

CONTENTS

KEY

 Creation mythology

 Gods and spirits

 Epic heroes and adventures

 Magical creatures

 Life and love

 Destruction and death

Ancient Greeks

- **We know about Greek mythology** from works of art and writings from as early as 800BC.

- **The earliest Ancient Greeks**, Bronze Age farmers, worshipped a Mother Earth goddess called Gaea.

- **Myths say** that Gaea emerged out of an emptiness called Chaos.

- **Gaea gave birth** to Ourea (Mountains), Pontus (Sea) and Uranus (Father Sky).

- **The next rulers** were the children of Gaea and Uranus: 12 immortals called the Titans.

◀ *In early Greek artworks, the Sphynx is a monster with a man's head, a lion's body and wings. Later artworks picture the Sphynx with a woman's head and chest.*

- **The children** of two Titans, Oceanus and Tethys, lived as spirits called nymphs in all the springs, rivers and seas of the world.

- **Another two Titans**, Cronus and Rhea, had children who overthrew them. These were the next immortal rulers: the Greek gods and goddesses.

- **Three Greek gods** divided the universe between them: Zeus ruled the earth, Poseidon ruled the seas, and Hades ruled the underworld kingdoms of the dead.

- **Some myths** say that the most intelligent Titan, Prometheus, created the first man out of clay and water.

- **Other Greek myths** say that the chief god, Zeus, has created five races of human beings. These are known as the Gold Race, the Silver Race, the Bronze Race, the Race of Heroes and the Race of Iron.

Scandinavian stories

- **Norse mythology** comes from people who lived in Scandinavia in the Bronze Age. These were the ancestors of the Vikings.

- **Myths say** that in the beginning was a huge emptiness called Ginnungagap. A fiery southern land called Muspellheim first came into existence, then a freezing northern land called Niflheim.

- **The fires eventually** began to melt the ice, and the dripping waters formed into the first being: a wicked Frost Giant named Ymir. More Frost Giants were formed from Ymir's sweat.

- **The next being** that grew from the thawed ice was a cow called Audhumla. Audhumla licked an ice block into a male being called Buri.

- **Buri's grandchildren** were the first three Norse gods: Odin, Vili and Ve. They killed Ymir and threw his body into Ginnungagap. His flesh, blood, bones, hair, skull and brains became the earth, seas, mountains, forests, sky and clouds.

- **Dwarves came into** existence before human beings. They grew from maggots in Ymir's flesh.

- **Odin, Vili and Ve** created the first man, Ask, from an ash tree and the first woman, Embla, from an elm tree. The gods gave humans a world called Midgard.

- **The gods tried** to keep the evil giants away by giving them a separate land, Jotunheim.

- **The gods built** themselves a heavenly homeland called Asgard.

- **A rainbow bridge** links the realm of the gods to the world of humans. Only gods could cross.

▶ *The rainbow bridge which linked Midgard to Asgard was known as Bifrost.*

Mesopotamia

- **Myths from the Middle East** are the oldest recorded mythology in the world, dating from 2500BC.

- **The Babylonian creation** myth grew from the Sumerian creation myth. It is called the Enuma Elish.

- **Every spring, Babylon was in danger** of flooding from the Tigris and Euphrates. Historians think that the Enuma Elish might have been acted out to please Marduk so he kept order and prevented the flooding.

▼ Around 2100BC, the Sumerians of Mesopotamia built massive stepped temples of mud-bricks called ziggurats.

- **The Enuma Elish** says that originally the universe was made of salt waters (Mother Tiamat), sweet waters, (Father Apsu) and a mist (their son Mummu).

- **The waters gave birth** to new young rebellious gods who overthrew Apsu and Mummu.

- **Tiamat and her** followers (led by a god called Kingu) were conquered by a male Babylonian god, Marduk, in a battle of powerful magic.

- **The Babylonians** pictured Marduk with four eyes and ears, so he could see and hear everything.

- **Marduk became** the new ruler. He made Tiamat's body into the earth and sky.

- **Human beings** were created out of Kingu's blood. Marduk made them build a temple to himself and the other gods at Babylon.

- **The Enuma Elish** was found written in a language called cuneiform on seven clay tablets by archaeologists excavating Nineveh in AD1845.

Ancient Egyptians

- **The mythology of Ancient Egypt** may go back to 4000BC when the land was used by farming peoples.

- **Folk in each area of Egypt** originally worshipped their own gods. Their stories spread and merged, so there are many versions and some gods are known in different forms.

- **Egyptian myths** say that in the beginning the universe was filled with dark waters.

- **The first god was Ra-Atum**. He appeared from the waters as the land of Egypt appears every year out of the flood waters of the Nile.

- **Ra-Atum spat** and the spittle turned into the gods Shu (air) and Tefnut (moisture).

- **Humans were created** one day when Shu and Tefnut wandered into the dark wastes and got lost. Ra-Atum sent his eye to find them. When they were reunited, Ra-Atum's tears of joy turned into people.

- **The world was created** when Shu and Tefnut gave birth to two children: Nut – the sky, and Geb – the Earth.

- **Ancient Egyptians believed** that Ra-Atum originally lived in the world with humans. When he grew old, humans tried to rebel against him. Ra then went to live in the sky.

- **Egyptian myths** were written down in hieroglyphic writing. This was invented around 3000BC, when Upper Egypt and Lower Egypt united into one kingdom.

- **It was not until** the 1820s that experts worked out what hieroglyphs meant. Before that, we knew about Ancient Egyptian mythology from old writings in other languages.

◄ Here the sun god is holding an ankh in his right hand. This is the sign of life and the key to the Underworld.

South Pacific stories

- **The remote islands of the South Pacific,** such as Polynesia, Hawaii and Tahiti, were untouched by the rest of the world for thousands of years. Mythological beliefs remain strong there to this day.

- **European explorers took over many islands** in the nineteenth century. Some islanders believed that this was because they had failed to keep myths and rituals alive, so they started to write them down.

- **Myths from west Polynesia** say that in the beginning the creator god Tangaroa lived in a dark emptiness called Po.

- **Some stories say that Tangaroa** formed the world by throwing down rocks into the watery wastes.

◀ The powerful god Tangaroa is an important figure in the mythologies of many South Pacific islands.

- **Some myths say that Tangaroa** created humans when he made a leafy vine to give his messenger bird, Tuli, some shade – the leaves were people.

- **Other Polynesian myths** say that the world was created by the joining of Ao (light) and Po (darkness).

- **In New Zealand,** the two forces who joined together in creation were Earth Mother and Sky Father – Papa and Rangi.

- **According to stories from New Zealand,** Tangaroa was the father of fish and reptiles.

- **Other gods in myths from New Zealand are:** Haumia, father of plants; Rongo, father of crops; Tane, father of forests; Tawhiri, god of storm; Tu, father of humans.

- **Myths say that certain gods were more important** than others. These 'chief gods' vary from island to island, according to who the islanders believe they were descended from.

Aboriginal beliefs

- **The mythology** of Australia comes from wandering tribes of people collectively called Aborigines.

- **The creation mythology** of the Aborigines is called the Dreamtime.

- **There are various** Dreamtime stories, which came from different tribes.

- **Most Dreamtime mythology** says that in the beginning, the earth was just a dark plain.

- **Aborigines from central Australia** believed that their ancestors slept beneath the Earth, with the Sun, the Moon and the stars. Eventually the ancestors woke up and wandered about the Earth in the shapes of humans, animals and plants, shaping the landscape.

- **Tribes from the northeast** believed that everything was created by two female ancestors who came across the sea from the Land of the Dead.

- **A wise rainbow snake** plays an important part in many Dreamtime myths.

- **Myths from** central Australia say that people were carved out of animals and plants by their ancestors who then went back to sleep in rocks, trees or underground – where they are today.

- **Aborigines from** south eastern Australia believed heroes from the sky shaped the world and created people.

- **Aborigines believe** that even the harshest landscape is sacred because the life of the ancestors runs through it.

▶ Aborigines believe that their ancestors had magical powers of creation.

Native Americans

- **Native American myths** come from the first people to live in North America who walked from Asia *c.* 15,000 years ago when the continents were linked by ice.

- **Native Americans** settled in many different tribes. Each tribe had its own myths and legends.

- **Many Native American** myths say that when the world was created, humans and animals lived together.

- **Some Native American tribes believed** that all creation is ruled over by a supreme spirit.

- **Most tribes believed** that everything is part of one harmonious creation. Harming anything upsets the balance of the world.

- **The Iroquois** believed that Mother Earth fell into a lake from a land beyond the sky. The animals helped create the Sun, the Moon and stars.

- **According to the Algonquian**, the Earth was created by Michabo the Great Hare, from a grain of sand from the bottom of the ocean.

- **The Navajo people** believed that the first man and woman were created when four gods ordered the winds to blow life into two ears of corn.

- **The Maidu tribe believed** that the gods Kodoyanpe and Coyote floated on the surface of a vast expanse of water and one day decided to create the world.

- **In 1855, Henry Wadsworth Longfellow wrote an epic poem** called *The Song of Hiawatha*, about a real Native American hero.

▲ *The Iroquois tribe lived in an eastern area of North America now known as New York State.*

Who were the Celts?

- **After the Roman invasion** of Britain in the first century AD, the Celts lived mainly in Ireland, Scotland, Wales, Cornwall and northern France.

- **Celtic myths** were told as stories by poets called bards and priests called druids.

- **In Celtic creation** mythology, Ireland existed at the beginning of time and was the whole world.

- **According to** Celtic myth, the first people to settle in Ireland all died in a great flood.

- **The second race** of settlers were male and female gods called the Partholons. They fought off a race of invading monsters called the Formorians, before being wiped out by a plague.

- **Another race of gods** called the Nemedians then settled in Ireland, but were forced out by Formorian attacks.

- **Tribes called the Fir Bolgs** then invaded. These were humans who knew magic.

- **A wise, skilled race** of god-like people called the Tuatha De Danaan arrived and defeated the Fir Bolgs and the Formorians.

- **Finally, a race of humans** called the Children of Mil invaded Ireland. They were the ancestors of the Celts.

- **When the Children of Mil** settled in Ireland, the Tuatha De Danaan used their magic powers to vanish from human sight, but have stayed in Ireland to this day.

▲ *The Celts made tools, weapons, armour and jewellery from different metals. This heavy, twisted neckband is called a torque.*

Indian myths

- **People have lived in India** for thousands of years. Myths are still an important part of their culture and religions today.

- **The earliest Indians** were farmers who thought that Prithivi, the Earth, and Dyaus, the sky, were the parents of all gods and humans.

- **A warrior race called the Aryans** then invaded India. They believed a god called Varuna created the world by picturing everything in his eye, the Sun.

▲ The continuous interaction between the different linguistic, religious and social groups through the ages has resulted in a rich variety of Indian mythology.

- **Aryans believed that the storm god** Indra later took over as chief god, supported by human beings. He rearranged the universe by organizing the heavens and the seasons.

- **The Hindu religion grew** from Aryan beliefs. Hindus believe that one great spirit is in everything. This is Brahman, whom they worship as thousands of different gods.

- **The god who creates the world** is Brahma. He emerges from a lotus flower floating on the floodwaters of chaos and thinks everything into being.

- **The god Vishnu preserves** the balance of good and evil in the universe by being born on earth as a human from time to time, to help men and women.

- **The god Shiva** is the destroyer god. He combats demons and keeps the universe moving by dancing.

- **After each 1000 Great Ages**, Shiva destroys the world by fire and flood. He preserves the seeds of all life in a golden egg, which Brahma breaks open to begin the rebirth of creation.

▲ The creator god Brahma is shown looking in all directions with four heads, to show that he has knowledge of all things.

> ★ STAR FACT ★
> Hindu mythology says the world is created, destroyed and re-created in cycles that go on for ever.

Chinese myths

- **The Chinese myths we know** may not be the oldest Chinese stories. Certain emperors in the past burned or rewrote many ancient books and traditional tales.

- **Certain myths tell** that the first people were created from wet clay by a mother goddess called Nugua.

- **There are many Chinese creation myths**. The most common story says that in the beginning the universe was an egg containing a mass of chaos.

- **Most myths say** that the first being was a dwarf-like creature called Panku, who pushed open the egg.

- **Many Chinese people believe** that everything in the universe has the force of either: Yin (the female, negative force of the Earth); or Yang (the male, positive force of the sky).

- **Myths say that Panku grew and grew** every day for 18,000 years, pushing the sky and Earth apart.

- **Some stories say that Panku then fell asleep** and died. Everything in the world was born from his body.

- **Other stories say that Panku remained alive** and carved everything in the world.

- **According to an ancient writing** called the Shu Ching, eight rulers created the universe together. These were the Three Sovereigns and the Five Emperors.

- **Many legends explain** that it is the duty of the ruler of China to keep order and balance in the universe in heaven as well as on Earth.

▶ Many Chinese creation myths, say Panku played a vital role in shaping the world.

Early Japanese myths

- **The earliest people to live in Japan** were called the Ainu. They believed that in the beginning the world was a swampy mixture of water and earth.

- **According to Ainu myth**, a creator god called Kamui sent a water wagtail to the swamp. This fluttered its wings and and tail, and islands appeared.

- **The Ainu believed** that people and animals were created by Kamui to live on the islands.

- **During the second and first centuries** BC people from Asia arrived in Japan. They brought a religion called Shinto.

- **Shinto myths say the world** was at first an ocean of chaos, which divided into light heavens above and heavy Earth below.

- **Shinto mythology says the first god** was like a reed shoot growing in the space between heaven and Earth.

- **Shinto beliefs say that a female god** called Izanami and a male god called Izanagi gave shape to the world. They stood on the rainbow and Izanagi stirred the ocean with a spear. An island formed, and the two gods left heaven to go and live on it.

- **The Shinto creation myth** says Japan was formed when Izanami gave birth to eight children who became islands.

- **Izanami and Izanagi** had many other children. These were the gods that shaped and then lived in every aspect of nature: the winds, seas, rivers, trees and mountains.

- **The ruler of the universe** is the sun goddess, Amaterasu. She was born from Izanagi's left eye.

▲ In the religion of Shinto, priests make offerings to the spirits of nature.

Tales from Africa

- **Numerous** tribal groups have lived in Africa for thousands of years, all with their own different myths and legends, although many shared beliefs.

- **Most African tribes believe** in one supreme creator god (who judges people wisely) and many minor gods.

- **Many myths say** that the creator god grew weary of constant demands from people, so he left the Earth and went to live in heaven.

- **The Yoruba people** of Nigeria believed that in the beginning the universe consisted of the sky, ruled by the chief god Olorun, and a watery marshland, ruled by the goddess Olokun.

- **The Yoruba believed** that a god called Obatala shaped the Earth with the help of magic gifts from other gods.

- **The Fon people** of Benin believed that the world was made by the moon goddess Mawu and her twin brother Lisa, the Sun.

- **The Dogon people** of Mali believed that the creator god moulded the Sun, Moon, Earth and people out of clay.

- **The Pygmies believed** that the first man and woman were brought forth by a chameleon who released them from a tree in a gush of water.

- **The Yoruba believed** that the chief god, Olorun, breathed life into the first people, who were modelled from mud.

▶ *The Fon people of Benin, where this sculpture comes from, were known from the early 17th century for their battle skills. Male warriors fought with a female army.*

> ★ STAR FACT ★
> Different tribal names for the creator god include Mulungu, Leza, Amma and Nyambe.

Who were the Maya?

- **The Maya were a great race** who lived in modern-day Guatemala, Honduras and Yucatan, 500BC–AD1524.

- **The Mayan creation story** is written in an ancient document called the Popol Vuh.

- **The Maya believed that in the beginning** there was nothing but darkness, with sky above and sea below.

- **Myths say that a group of gods** together shaped the landscape and formed animals and birds.

- **The Popol Vuh explains** that the first two human races made by the Creators were not good enough and had to be destroyed.

- **The first successful people** were made out of corn, at the suggestion of a jaguar, coyote, crow and a parrot.

- **The Maya believe that the third race** of humans were so perfect they were almost as good as the Creators themselves. So the Creators clouded the intelligence of the humans so they could no longer see the gods.

- **The Maya believed that they could** get back in touch with the gods by taking certain mind-altering drugs.

- **The Maya believed that when humans** were created the world was still in darkness. People begged for light, so the Creators made the Sun, Moon and stars.

▼ *The Maya built huge stone temples and palaces in the shape of pyramids, like this one at Teotihuacan.*

> ★ STAR FACT ★
> As in the Christian creation story in the Bible, the Popol Vuh says that women were created after men.

South American stories

- **Most South American myths** we know come from the Inca race, who built a great empire in Peru from the thirteenth century AD until they were conquered by Spanish invaders in 1532.

- **Inca means 'children of the sun'**. Some South American myths say that the sun was created on an island in Lake Titicaca.

- **Inca mythology grew from ancient tales** told by tribal peoples who had lived in Peru from around 2500BC.

- **A pre-Inca Tiahuanaco myth** tells that in the beginning a god called Con Ticci Viracocha emerged out of nothingness and created everything.

- **Con Ticci Viracocha** is said to have later returned to earth out of Lake Titicaca, destroyed his world in a huge flood, and created everything again.

- **Another myth tells how the first humans** were created by a boneless man called Con, who was the son of the sun. He was later overthrown by another child of the sun, Pachacamac, who created a new race of people.

- **An ancient coastal tribe in Peru** believed in a creator god called Coniraya. They believed he had filled the sea with fish and taught them how to farm the land.

- **The Canaris tribe believed they were descended** from an ancient parrot or macaw, who had bred with the few survivors of a terrible flood.

- **The Inca believe** they magically appeared one day from a place called Paccari-tambo, which means 'inn of origin'.

- **Myths say** that the first Incas were led by eight royal gods: four brothers and four sisters.

▶ This statue was created by the Tiahuanaco people of Peru. This important civilization lived in the highlands around Lake Titicaca before the Incas invaded.

▲ These modern-day Peruvians are fishing on Lake Titicaca – an important site in Inca myth.

Toltec and Aztec tales

- **The Toltecs were** a civilization in Mexico between AD900 and 1200. The Aztecs were a race of warriors who came to power in 1376.

- **The Toltecs built huge pyramid** temples that still stand, covered in pictures of their myths.

▲ *These Toltec ruins, known today as El Castillo, date from eleventh century AD.*

- **We know about Aztec myths** from an ancient Aztec calendar, and a document that explains how Aztec gods fit into the calendar.

- **Toltecs and Aztecs** believed that humans and gods needed to make sacrifices to keep the universe alive.

- **In the beginning**, the gods created and destroyed four worlds one after another, because humans did not make enough sacrifices.

- **In order to create a sun** for the fifth world, two gods sacrificed themselves by jumping into a bonfire.

- **At first the fifth world** consisted only of water with a female monster goddess floating in it, eating everything. The mighty gods Quetzalcoatl and Tezcatlipoca ripped the goddess apart and turned her body into the earth and the heavens.

- **The Aztecs believed that the sun** god and the earth monster needed sacrifices of human blood and hearts in order to remain fertile and alive.

- **Human beings were created** by Quetzalcoatl, from his blood and the powdered bones of his dead father.

- **Quetzalcoatl and Tezcatlipoca** brought musicians and singers from the House of the Sun down to Earth. Living things could then create their own music.

Beliefs from Persia

> **★ STAR FACT ★**
> Persia is the ancient name for modern-day Iran.

- **We know many of Persia's myths and legends** from a document called the Shah name or Book of Kings, written by a poet called Firdausi around AD1000.

- **An Ancient Persian myth** says that in the beginning there was a flat mass of earth and water. Then evil came through the sky, stirring up the landscape.

- **According to early myth**, Persia was at the world's centre. Mount Alburz grew for 800 years until its peak touched the heavens. At its base was a gate to hell.

- **The earliest Persian gods** were good and evil forces of nature, such as Vayu (wind god who brought life-giving rain) and Apaosha (demon of drought).

- **Much of Persia's mythology** comes from a religion founded by a prophet called Zoroaster in the sixth century BC.

- **According to Zoroastrianism**, the world began when Ahura Mazda created time. He gave birth to everything that is good: light, love, justice and peace.

- **Evil entered the universe** when Ahura Mazda's jealous twin, Ahriman, attacked the world.

- **Ahriman killed Gayomart**, but Ahura Mazda created a new human couple, Mashya and Mashyoi. He left them free to worship either himself or the wicked Ahriman, as humans have been free to do ever since.

- **The first human** was a man called Gayomart. Ahura Mazda created him from light.

▶ *The people of Persia followed the teachings of the prophet Zoroaster (top right), from the sixth to the seventh century BC.*

Greeks and Romans

- **The Greek gods and goddesses** have very human qualities. They act out of love and hate, as we do.

- **Myths say that giants called the Cyclops** gave Zeus the gift of thunder and lightning, and Poseidon the gift of a fishing spear called a trident, with which he could stir up sea-storms, tidal waves and earthquakes.

- **The gods were believed to have taught humans** life-skills: Zeus – justice, Poseidon – ship-building, Hestia – home-making, and Demeter – farming.

- **Gods** (except for Artemis) opposed human sacrifice and cannibalism. Zeus once punished King Lycaon for eating human flesh by turning him into a wolf.

- **The Greek gods and goddesses** sometimes fell in love with humans. Their children were heroes, such as Heracles and Perseus.

- **The gods and goddesses of Ancient Greece** were adopted by the Romans, under new names. Hence Zeus became Jove, Hera became Juno, and so on.

- **The stories about Greek and Roman gods**, spirits and heroes are known as Classical mythology.

- **The Ancient Greeks and Romans** believed that spirits called dryads lived inside trees.

- **In Latin, the language of the Romans**, 'templum' means the space where a shrine to a god was erected. This is where we get our word temple from.

- **Greeks and Romans** would sometimes leave small offerings at the shrine of a god. These could be food, flowers, money or sweet-smelling incense.

▶ *The Greek sea god Poseidon, whose Roman name is Neptune, held a trident with which he could stir up waves into terrible sea-storms.*

The Titans

- **The Titans were 12 immortals** in Greek and Roman mythology.

- **The strongest of the Titans** was Atlas – he held up the sky. The cleverest was Prometheus.

- **A Titan called Epimetheus** is said to have married the first mortal woman, Pandora.

- **The Titan Helios became god of the Sun**. Selene became goddess of the Moon.

- **Oceanus became god of the river** that the Greeks believed surrounded the Earth.

- **Themis became goddess** of prophecies at a city called Delphi.

▶ *After the war between the gods and the Titans, the god Zeus punished the Titan Atlas by commanding him to hold up the skies on his shoulders.*

- **A prophecy said** that the youngest Titan, Cronus, would be overthrown by his own son. So when Cronus's children were born, he ate them. However, his wife hid one child away – this was Zeus.

- **When Zeus was grown up**, he fed Cronus a cup of poison which caused him to vomit up all the other children he had swallowed. These emerged as the fully grown gods and goddesses: Poseidon, Hades, Hera, Demeter and Hestia.

- **Zeus and his brothers** and sisters fought against the Titans for ten years. The Titans were finally overthrown when the gods and goddesses secured the help of the Hundred-handed Giants and Cyclopes.

- **The Titans were hurled** into an underworld realm of punishment called Tartarus. There, they were bound in chains for ever.

Norse warrior gods

- **Ancient Norse peoples** told stories about a race of gods and goddesses called the Aesir. They were brave warriors, just like the Vikings themselves.

- **Odin, the chief of the warrior gods**, has a high throne called Lidskialf, from which he can see everything.

- **The Norse gods** do not take much notice of humans. They are more concerned with battling giants and dealing with other magical creatures.

- **Odin** likes to disguise himself as a traveller and wander undetected through the world of humans.

- **Norse gods and goddesses** are not immortal. They can be killed by cunning magic or simple bravery.

- **The most important warrior** goddesses are Odin's wife, Frigg (a mother goddess with fertility powers) and the beautiful Freya (goddess of love).

- **The daughters of Odin** were spirits called Valkyries. They flew over battlefields and took dead brave warriors to live in Valhalla in Asgard.

- **Two days of the week are named** after Norse warrior gods. Wednesday means Woden's Day – Woden was another name for Odin, father of the gods. Thursday means Thor's Day – Norse god of thunder.

- **The Aesir once fought** against gods and goddesses called the Vanir (or 'shining ones'). They finally made a peaceful alliance against the giants.

- **The ruler of the Vanir** was the fertility god Njord, ruler of the winds and the sea.

◄ Norse stories are the mythology of the Vikings – seafaring warriors from Norway, Sweden and Denmark who invaded other parts of Europe.

The gods of Egypt

- **The mighty sun god**, Ra-Atum, was called many different names by Ancient Egyptians.

- **The sun god was sometimes pictured** as a scarab beetle, because a scarab beetle rolls a ball of dung before it, as the ball of the Sun rolls across the sky.

- **Myths say that the sun god** has a secret name, known only to himself, which was the key to all his power.

- **The Ancient Egyptians believed** that part of a god's spirit could live on Earth in the body of an animal. This is why gods are pictured as humans with animal heads.

◄ The blue scarab beetle Khephri is one of the many forms of the sun god. This amulet was made over 3000 years ago.

- **Hathor or Sekhmet** was the daughter and wife of Ra-Atum. She could take on the form of a terrifying lioness or cobra to attack enemies of the sun god.

- **Osiris was the son of Ra-Atum**. He became king of Egypt and, later, ruler of the underworld Kingdom of the Dead.

- **Osiris's brother, Seth**, represented evil in the universe. He hatched a wicked plot to murder Osiris and take the crown of Egypt for himself.

- **Osiris's sister and wife** was called Isis. She was a powerful mother goddess of fertility.

- **Horus was Osiris's son**. He inherited the throne of Egypt. Ancient Egyptians believed that all pharaohs were descended from Horus, and were therefore gods.

- **An amulet is a piece of jewellery** with magical powers. Many amulets were in the shape of an eye – either the sun god's or Horus's. The sacred eye was thought to have healing powers and to ward off evil.

Native American spirits

- **Many Native Americans** believed they could trace their families back through legends to a particular animal or bird. They made carvings (totems) of these creatures, to help them contact the spirits of their ancestors.

- **Many tribes believed** that they would be punished by the animal spirits of their ancestors if they hunted or fished for more food than they needed.

- **Four sky spirits were** important to the Pawnee: the North Star (their creator), the Morning Star (their protector), the South Star (the underworld leader of enemy forces), and the Evening Star (bringer of darkness).

- **Central tribes believed that** Sedna was the Old Woman of the Sea. She controlled sea creatures and caused storms.

- **Stories of the Algonquian** tribe say that all things in nature which are helpful to humans were the idea of a god called Gluskap. All hostile, poisonous natural things are the work of his brother, Malsum.

- **South Eastern tribes** including the Cherokee built earth mounds in the shape of sacred animal spirits, around which all tribal ceremonies were held.

◄ *Native Americans carved pictures of the spirits of their ancestors into whole tree trunks, known today as totem poles.*

- **The Arikara people of the plains** believed that the Corn Mother taught them agriculture and that they could keep peace by making offerings of smoke to the Sky Spirit.

- **Shamans or 'medicine men'** were holy men who knew how to contact spirits. They sometimes used herbs and chanting to sink into a trance, allowing a spirit to enter them and speak.

- **In the late nineteenth century** many Native American tribes performed ghost dances to ask the spirits of their animal ancestors to drive European settlers from their lands.

> ★ **STAR FACT** ★
> The Iroquois believed that all spirits were ruled over by a guardian called the Great Manitou.

▼ *European settlers in North America fought Native American tribes for their land. By 1890, the tribes had all been pushed onto few and far-between reservations.*

Hindu deities

- **Hindus believe that one day** in the life of the supreme spirit, Brahman, is equivalent to 4320 million years on Earth.

- **Hindus believe** that there is a set, correct way for everyone to behave, according to their role in society. Myths say that the god Vishnu established this code of good behaviour on earth, known as 'dharma'.

- **The wife of the mighty destroyer god**, Shiva, is a very important goddess. She has three forms: the gentle Parvati, the brave demon-fighter Durga, and bloodthirsty Kali.

- **Ganesha is the popular Hindu god** of wisdom. He is pictured with an elephant's head.

- **The Hindu word for temple is 'mandir'**. Worship is 'puja'.

- **Hindus believe that gods and goddesses** are present in their shrines and temples. The picture or statue that represents them living there is known as a murti.

◀ Hindu temples are ornately decorated with statues and carvings of the gods.

- **When Hindus worship at a shrine** or temple, they leave the god or goddess an offering of food or flowers.

- **In Hindu art, gods and goddesses** are often painted blue – the Hindu colour of holiness.

- **Hindu gods and goddesses** are often pictured with several heads or arms, to show their special characteristics.

- **In 1995, thousands of people in India** reported that statues of Hindu gods were drinking milk. Some believed this was a miracle. Others said the statues were made of porous stone that soaked up the liquid.

Chinese divinities

- **For many years**, the Chinese have worshipped spirits of dead ancestors, believing they can help the living.

- **The first emperors** in China ruled over warrior tribes and belonged to a family called the Shang dynasty (around 1500–1050BC). They were believed to be gods, as were all following emperors.

- **According to many myths**, the first Shang emperor is the most powerful of all Chinese gods. He is known as the Jade Emperor.

- **The Jade Emperor's wife** was a goddess who grew Peaches of Immortality in her palace gardens. They only ripened once every 6000 years.

▶ Chinese emperors kept the vast country cut off from the rest of the world until the nineteenth century.

- **The first Chinese man to die** and find the Underworld became chief god of the dead, Yen-Lo Wang.

- **The Chinese believe that their homes** are guarded by special spirits. Tsao Chun is the god of the kitchen. He reports on each family to heaven.

- **As in other civilizations**, through the centuries many real Chinese heroes were often appointed to be gods, thousands of years after their deaths.

- **Kuan Ti lived in the third century** AD and became famous as one of China's finest warriors. He was made a war god, to defend China from enemies.

- **Wen Chang was an outstanding** student who lived in the third or fourth century AD. He was made god of literature.

- **Wen Chang has an assistant god**, Kuei Hsing, whom people pray to for help in exams. Stories say that he was once a very gifted scholar, but incredibly ugly!

Immortals of Japan

- **Myths of the early Japanese** do not tell of a supreme spirit. Instead, they suggest that a divine force flows through all nature in the form of millions of gods.

- **The storm god Raiden** got his name from two Japanese words: 'rai' (thunder) and 'den' (lightning).

- **Susano was the god of seas and oceans.** He was banished from heaven and sent to live in the Underworld.

- **Inari was the god of crops.** He is pictured as a bearded man holding sheaves of rice and riding on a fox.

- **Over time**, nature gods grew as warrior heroes, religious leaders and emperors became gods.

- **In the sixth century**, a religion called Buddhism was introduced into Japan and a pantheon of Japanese Buddhist gods and goddesses developed.

- **In Japanese Buddhism**, Amida is the god of a paradise for the dead. He has two helpers, Kwannon, the goddess of mercy, and Shishi, the lord of might.

- **Japanese myth says that there are about 500** immortal men and women called Sennin who live in the mountains. They can fly and work powerful magic.

- **A Shishi is a spirit pictured** as a cross between a dog and a lion. It is believed to ward off evil demons.

- **There are seven Japanese gods of luck** called Shichi Fukujin, meaning 'seven happiness beings'.

◀ The religion of Buddhism spread to Japan from India. Worshippers follow the teachings of the Buddha, or 'enlightened one'.

The Persian pantheon

- **The earliest Persians** worshipped nature deities such as Tishtrya, god of fertility, and Anahita, goddess of the lakes and oceans.

- **Three famous priests** of the nature god cult were the Magi – the three wise men or kings who visited Jesus.

- **In ancient times**, the god of victory, Verethragna, was worshipped widely through the Persian empire by soldiers.

- **The human heroes** of Persian myths and legends were also worshipped as god-like rulers.

- **In the first and second century**, the god of light, Mithras, became an important deity. He was another warrior hero who protected creation by killing forces of evil.

- **From the sixth century**, the beliefs of a prophet called Zoroaster spread through Persia. In this religion, Zoroastrianism, the ancient gods became saints called Yazatas.

- **The chief god in Zoroastrianism**, Ahura Mazda, was later known as Ohrmazd.

- **Ahura Mazda was said to be Zoroaster's** father. Zoroaster's mother was believed to be a virgin.

- **According to Zoroaster**, creation is protected by seven spirit guardians known as Amesha Spentas.

- **Zoroastrians believe that everyone** is looked after by a guardian spirit, or Fravashi. These spirits represent the good in people and help those who ask.

▶ One Persian myth says that the god Mithras brought fertility to the world by killing a bull, which contained all the strength of the Earth, and sprinkling its blood over the land.

Celtic religion

- **Centuries before Christianity**, the Celtic peoples of the Great Britain, Ireland and Northern France, were led in worship of their gods by priests called Druids.

- **The name 'Druid' comes from** the Celtic word 'druidh', which is connected with the Greek word for oak, 'drus'. The oak was a sacred symbol.

- **Celts in different places called their gods** different names and worshipped them in different forms.

- **Many myths tell of a horned god** who leads a terrifying wild hunt across the sky.

- **An important race of gods** and goddesses, the Tuatha De Danann, had a chief called the Dagda. He was the lord of magic, knowledge, the weather and fire.

- **Another great leader** of the Tuatha De Danann was the warrior god Nuada.

  ▶ *Around 2000BC early Celts built a circle of enormous stones on Salisbury Plain in England. Some historians think it may have been used for worshipping the sun. It is known today as Stonehenge.*

- **The hero Lugh was master of all skills**, including magic. After many deeds, he became an immortal.

- **Three important goddesses** of battle and death: the cruel Morrigan; the goddess of Ulster, Macha; and Badb, who sometimes took the form of a raven.

- **A Celtic god known today as 'the Green Man'** was carved into early Christian churches across the British Isles and Europe, representing the power of nature.

- **In England, traditional Morris dances** re-enact Celtic springtime celebrations. Morris men leap into the air as a symbol of life triumphing over death.

Sacrifices for gods

◀ *The wealthy backer of a Roman gladiatorial games often dedicated the deaths of the gladiators to his or her favourite god or goddess.*

- **The Maya used to play** a ball-game a bit like football. Historians think that at the end of the match, one side was sacrificed to the gods.

- **The Hindu god** Shiva's first wife was Sati. Sati's father tried to disgrace Shiva, and in protest, Sati sacrificed herself by throwing herself onto a sacred fire.

- **The chief Norse god, Odin**, demanded that warriors did not just give themselves up to death fearlessly, but that they actually welcomed death, in his honour.

- **The ancient Hindu fire god**, Agni, had seven tongues to lick up sacrifices of butter burnt on a sacred fire.

- **A Bible story** tells how God asked Abraham to offer him his only son, Isaac, as a sacrifice. God stopped Abraham in time, once he had tested his obedience.

- **A sacred fire** to the Roman goddess Vesta was tended by specially chosen girls called the Vestal Virgins. They sacrificed having boyfriends or getting married.

- **In Native American tribes**, dancers wearing 'false face masks' to ward off evil spirits often made offerings of food and 'corn animals' to the good spirits in nature.

- **Thousands of people** were sacrificed at a time to the Aztec sun god Huitzilopochtli.

- **The Romans** often offered the deaths of gladiators to honour a particular god or goddess.

- **Druid priests** sometimes made sacrifices to the Celtic gods by hanging up criminals or prisoners of war in big wicker cages and burning them alive.

Gifts from gods

- **In Greek myth**, when Perseus went to kill the Gorgon, the gods gave him a helmet of invisibility, winged sandals, and a highly polished bronze shield.

- **Egyptian myth says that** the god Osiris taught people the skill of farming and gave laws and religious rites.

- **A French story** says that Joan of Arc heard God telling her to go into an ancient church and dig behind the altar. She found a sword used in the Crusades.

- **In Greek myth,** Athena gave Bellerophon a golden bridle to catch the magical winged horse, Pegasus.

- **A Japanese myth** says that when the sun goddess, Amaterasu, was hiding in a cave, the other gods enticed her out with the gift of the first ever mirror.

- **Inuit myths** tell how it was the raven who brought many gifts to humans.

- **In Greek myth,** Thetis knew her son, Achilles, would die in the Trojan Wars. She protected him with armour made by the gods' blacksmith, Hephaestus.

- **A Christian story says** that when Jesus was on his way to die on the cross, a woman called Veronica wiped his bleeding face. The imprint of Jesus's features was left on her handkerchief.

- **Greek myth says** that King Midas asked the gods for 'the golden touch'– anything he touched was turned into gold. He regretted it when he tried to eat.

- *The Ramayana* **tells how the great god Indra** gave the monkey hero Hanuman the power to choose his own death, as a gift for helping Prince Rama.

▶ *Greedy King Midas won the gift of 'the golden touch' – but ended up begging the gods to take it back.*

Making mischief

- **In Native American myths**, the trickster god Coyote is usually up to no good. However, he sometimes uses his cunning to help the human race.

- **The Polynesian god Maui** is one of the greatest mischief-makers in all mythologies. Like Coyote, he too uses his tricks to help humans.

- **Kobolds were a type of earth-spirit** or dwarf said to live in German silver mines. They enjoyed causing trouble for human miners, such as explosions.

- **The Aborigines of Arnhem Land** in the Northern Territory of Australia believe in

  ▶ *Every leprechaun is believed to have a secret stash of hidden gold.*

rock spirits called Mimi. The Mimi can be kind, but if strangers disturb them, they cause severe illnesses.

- **Stories from the Caribbean** tell of a fun-loving half-man, half-spider character called Anansi. He loves to create havoc for his arch-enemy, Tiger.

- **In Japanese mythology** spirits of the dead often cause trouble for those who hurt them while they were alive.

- **Some people believe that the power** of the Celtic god Lug dwindled away until he became a mischievous sprite called a 'lugh-chromain' or leprechaun.

- **In Eastern European myth**, a kikimora is a female house spirit. If the house is kept dirty, the kikimora will whine and whistle.

- **In World War II**, fighter pilots and plane engineers blamed sprites, Gremlins, for things that went wrong with aircraft.

Tricks played on gods

◄ *The Egyptian goddess Isis knew such powerful magic that she once tricked the great sun god, Ra-Atum.*

- **Native American Algonquian** myth says that the god Gluskap thought he was so great that there was no one in the universe who would not obey him. A woman defeated his boast by bringing him her baby!

- **The Egyptian goddess Isis** created a poisonous snake to bite the sun god. She said she would only cure him if he told her his secret name, so giving her his power.

- **In Norse mythology**, prophecies said that a mighty wolf called Fenris would kill the chief god, Odin. The gods tricked Fenris into being tied up with a rope.

- **The Tupinamba people** of South America once thought that a great shaman, Maira-Monan, was growing too powerful. They killed him by tricking him into walking into a fire of powerful magic.

- **Osiris, the great God of Egypt**, was secretly murdered in a trick by his jealous brother, Seth. Seth coaxed Osiris into a coffin, then slammed the lid shut.

- **According to Greek myth**, the Titan Prometheus tricked the chief god Zeus into accepting just animal bones and fat from humans as sacrifices.

- **A Native American myth** tells how the god Coyote tried to smoke a rabbit out of his burrow. The rabbit turned the trick, by hurling the fire out at the god!

- **In Chinese myth** the Jade Emperor once made Monkey the Keeper of the Heavenly Horse. In fact, Monkey was just a stable boy!

- **South Pacific islands myths** tell of the god Maui who tried to trick a goddess called Hina into granting immortality to the world. Hina killed Maui.

- **Norse myth says that the blind god** Hodur was tricked into killing his twin brother Baldur, loved by all creation. The start of the end for the warrior gods.

Gilgamesh

- **This epic poem is from Sumeria** – one of the earliest civilizations to have city states, laws and irrigation.

- **Gilgamesh was a real king** of the Sumerian city Uruk, around 2700–2500BC.

- **In the poem, King Gilgamesh** is a man of mighty strength who is loved dearly by the gods.

- **When the nobles of Uruk** complain to the gods that King Gilgamesh is a tyrant, the Mother Goddess makes a hero called Enkidu to challenge him. Gilgamesh meets his match in Enkidu, and the two become firm friends.

- **When Enkidu dies**, Gilgamesh begins to fear his own death. He embarks on a quest to find out how to become immortal.

- **Gilgamesh does not win eternal life**, but is rewarded with a plant which will keep him young and strong for the rest of his days. When a watersnake steals it from him, he nearly despairs.

- **Gilgamesh finally realizes** that the only type of immortality humans can achieve is fame through great deeds and building lasting monuments.

- **The poem was found in 1845**, when archaeologists were excavating at the ancient city of Nineveh.

- **Experts think that** *Gilgamesh* was first written down on clay tablets in an ancient language – cuneiform. It is the earliest recorded major work of literature.

- **Fragments of** *Gilgamesh* have been found by archaeologists in ancient sites throughout many countries of the Middle East.

▲ *This ancient Sumerian stone relief shows the hero Gilgamesh as the central figure.*

The oral tradition

- **Myths and legends existed** in civilizations all over the world for thousands of years before writing was developed. They were told as entertainment by professional poets specially trained to remember the long works and perform them out loud. This is called the oral tradition of literature.

- **An epic is an adventure story** in the form of a long poem, which follows the brave deeds of a human hero as he struggles against magical dangers.

- **The heroes of many epics** are often born into royalty and brought up away from their parents.

- **Many epic heroes** possess superhuman powers and are helped by gods or spirits.

- **Most epic heroes** possess at least one magical weapon or object with magic powers.

- **Epic poetry provided** early peoples with standards and goals for how to live a good life.

◀ One of the enduring Greek stories is of Daedalus, whose son Icarus flew too close to the sun, melting the wax on the wings that had been crafted for him to escape from King Minos.

- **The most famous epics** are the Greek poems *The Iliad* and *The Odyssey*. Some historians think these were written by a blind man called Homer around 750BC. Others think they were composed gradually in the oral tradition by a series of poets.

- **Archaeologists have found** written fragments of *The Iliad* and *The Odyssey* dating from the fourth century BC. However, the oldest complete manuscripts are dated from the tenth century AD.

- **Medieval poets were called bards** or troubadors. They often chanted their tales to music.

▼ The crews of these Ancient Greek triremes sailed off to do battle with ships and lands taking with them their stories of legends and myths.

> **★ STAR FACT ★**
> The name for traditional storytellers in some parts of Africa was griots.

Heracles's labours

- **Heracles was Zeus's son** by a mortal woman. Zeus's divine wife, Hera, was so jealous that she would only allow Zeus to make Heracles immortal if Heracles could complete a series of impossible tasks.

- **Unlike other Greek heroes**, Heracles does not set out seeking fame, fortune and immortality. He performs the labours because it is commanded by the gods.

- **Two labours involved killing** terrifying beasts: the man-eating Nemean lion and a nine-headed, poisonous swamp monster called the Hydra.

- **Four labours involved** capturing magical creatures alive: the golden deer sacred to the goddess Artemis, the vicious Erymanthian boar, a ferocious bull belonging to the god Poseidon, and some flesh-eating horses.

- **One labour was to get rid** of a flock of birds who shot feathers like arrows.

- **Two labours involved stealing** precious objects: the belt of the fearsome Amazon queen, Hippolyte; and a herd of cattle belonging to the giant, Geryon.

- **A humiliating labour was** to clean out the biggest, dirtiest stables in the world.

- **The final labours required** journeying to the ends of the Earth to fetch some golden apples and venturing into the Underworld to bring back the three-headed guard dog, Cerberus.

- **After many adventures**, Heracles was finally poisoned. As he lay dying, Zeus took him up to Mount Olympus, at last to join the gods as an immortal.

- **In ancient times**, Heracles was the most popular Greek hero.

◀ *After Heracles killed the ferocious Nemean lion, he wore its pelt like a cloak for the rest of his days.*

Jason and the Argonauts

- **According to Ancient Greek** myth, Jason was a prince of Iolcus who was exiled from his home as a child when his uncle seized the throne.

- **A wise centaur called Chiron** brought up Jason with other abandoned future heroes, including the mighty warriors Achilles and Aeneas.

- **It was the centaur**, Chiron, who gave Jason his name. It means 'healer'.

- **Jason returned** to Iolchus to claim his throne. His uncle agreed to give it up if Jason went to the ends of the earth and brought back a magical Golden Fleece.

- **Jason built a huge ship** for the voyage, called the *Argo*. The goddess Athene gave a magic bough for the prow, which was able to speak words of advice.

- **The greatest heroes** in Greek mythology, including Heracles, volunteered to help Jason in his task. They became known as the Argonauts.

- **Jason and the Argonauts** faced many perils on their sea voyage, reworked into the epic poem, *The Odyssey*.

- **A beautiful witch-girl** called Medea fell in love with Jason. She used her magic to help Jason win the Golden Fleece from its owner and escape.

- **The name Medea** means 'cunning'.

- **Jason later left Medea**, breaking an oath to the gods, causing trouble. Some said that Medea murdered Jason in revenge. Others believed that he died an old beggar man.

▼ *One hazard encountered by Jason and the Argonauts on their voyage was the Symplegades. These were rocks which clashed together, crushing ships passing between them.*

Theseus's adventures

- **There are many myths** about a hero called Theseus who became king of Attica in Greece. Historians have proved that a real King Theseus did once exist.

- **According to legends**, Theseus, secret son of a king called Aegeus, was brought up away from Attica to keep him safe from those who wanted the throne.

- **As a young man**, Theseus travelled to Attica to claim his birthright. He chose a long route through many dangers, because he wanted to prove himself on the way.

- **Theseus once took** a mighty bronze-plated club from a thug who tried to kill him. He used the weapon for the rest of his life.

- **Theseus liked to punish criminals** by their own evil methods. One villain tied people between two bent young trees which sprang back and ripped them apart. He got a dose of his own medicine!

- **When Theseus reached Attica**, his father's new wife tried to poison him – Aegeus realized just in time.

- **Aegeus** sent young people as a sacrifice to King Minos of Crete. Thesesus volunteered to go. Thrown into a maze called the Labyrinth to be eaten by a bull-headed man, the Minotaur, he slew the monster.

- **King Minos's daughter**, Ariadne, fell in love with Theseus and helped him escape from the Labyrinth.

- **Archaeologists found** that the ancient royal palace of Crete was laid out like a maze and that a sport like bull-fighting was popular. The Minotaur myth may have arisen from this.

- **Historians credit Theseus** with building Athens as an important Greek centre of power.

▶ *Myth says that the Minotaur was created when the god Poseidon cruelly caused King Minos's wife to fall in love with a magnificent bull. Their affair resulted in a child with a human body and a bull's head.*

The Trojan War

◀ *This Ancient Greek vase shows the warrior Achilles. He was protected by divine armour – except for a small spot on his heel, where he received his death wound.*

- **The Iliad is an epic poem** that tells of events at the end of a ten-year war between the Ancient Greeks and Trojans.

- **The Trojan War** began when Paris, a Trojan nobleman, kidnapped Helen, Queen of Sparta. Her father asked the Greeks to help win her back.

- **When The Iliad was composed**, no written records about the Trojan War existed. The story was passed down by word of mouth for hundreds of years.

- **The city of Troy existed** as archaeologists have discovered its remains. The city burned in 1184BC.

- **The principal characters** in *The Iliad* are the noblemen of both sides. They aim to win fame by fighting honourably and dying a warrior's death.

- **The greatest Greek warrior** is Achilles. When he argues with the Greek commander, Agamemnon, and withdraws from battle, the Greek army suffers.

- **The greatest Trojan warrior** is Paris's brother, Hector.

- **Goddesses and gods play a major** role in *The Iliad*. They support different sides, giving their human favourites advice and help.

- **The Iliad is the earliest** written work from Ancient Greece.

- **The Greeks eventually won** the Trojan War. The hero Odysseus built a huge wooden horse, inside which many Greek warriors hid. The Greeks left it outside the gates of Troy and the Trojans took it inside the city, thinking it was a gift. At night, the Greek warriors scrambled out and destroyed the city.

Odysseus and The Odyssey

▲ One Greek legend says that the Sirens were so furious when Odysseus escaped their clutches that they drowned themselves.

- **The Odyssey is an adventure** story which follows the Greek hero, Odysseus, after the Trojan War, on his long and difficult sea voyage home.

- **Odysseus and his men** have to face many magical dangers on their journey, including monsters and giants.

- **On one occasion,** some of Odysseus's sailors eat lotus fruit, which makes them forget all about returning to their families and homes.

- **Odysseus has to sail safely** past the Sirens. These are half-woman, half-bird creatures who live on a craggy seashore. They sing a magical song that lures sailors to steer their ships onto the rocks to their deaths.

- **The goddess of war,** Athena, acts as Odysseus's patron, giving him special help and guidance.

▶ After 20 years at war, Odysseus returns to his kingdom disguised as a beggar. He is greeted by his old dog, who then dies content.

★ **STAR FACT** ★
Unlike its companion poem, *The Iliad*, *The Odyssey* has a happy ending.

- **The sea god Poseidon** hates Odysseus and seeks to shipwreck him.

- **By the time Odysseus finally** reaches his palace in Ithaca, he has been away for 20 years. Disguised as a beggar, only his faithful old dog recognizes him.

- **Once home, Odysseus's troubles** are not over. Powerful suitors are pressurizing his faithful wife, Penelope, for her hand in marriage, so they can seize Odysseus's crown.

- **Women often hold positions** of great power in the poem. For instance, Circe is a very powerful sorceress who turns some of Odysseus's sailors into pigs. The goddess Calypso keeps Odysseus captive on her island for seven years.

The Aeneid

◀ *According to one Ancient source, the poet Virgil was tall and dark with the appearance of a countryman.*

● **The Aeneid is an epic poem** which follows the adventures of a Trojan prince, Aeneas, after the end of the Trojan War.

● **The Aeneid was not composed** in the oral tradition. The Roman author, Virgil, wrote it down in Latin.

● **Virgil was the well-educated son** of a farmer. The Roman Emperor, Augustus Caesar, recognized his writing talent and became his patron .

● **Virgil based the legends** in his poem and its structure on the epics *The Iliad* and *The Odyssey*.

● **In *The Iliad*, Aeneas fights** many times against the Greeks, but is saved because he has another destiny.

● **It was popular in the sixth century** BC to picture part of the legend of Aeneas on vases – how he carried his father to safety out of the smoking ruins of Troy.

● **Virgil designed *The Aeneid*** to give Augustus and the Roman empire a glorious history. It explains that the gods themselves instructed Aeneas to travel to Italy, to be the ancestor of a great race – the Romans. It shows how Augustus Caesar was directly descended from the mighty hero.

● **In *The Aeneid*, Aeneas falls in love** with Queen Dido of Carthage and then abandons her, sailing for Italy. Virgil probably made up this myth to explain the hatred that existed between Rome and Carthage.

● **Virgil began *The Aeneid*** in 29BC and worked on it for the last ten years of his life. As he lay dying , he asked for the poem to be burnt, but Caesar overruled him.

● **A great Italian poet**, Dante Alighieri (1265–1321), used Virgil's style and the legends of *The Aeneid* as the basis for his own poem, the *Divine Comedy*.

Romulus and Remus

● **The story of Romulus and Remus** tells how twin boys grew up to build the foundations of the city of Rome.

● **Versions of the myth were written** by many great Roman writers, such as Livy, Plutarch and Virgil.

● **According to the legend**, Romulus and Remus were descendants of the hero Aeneas. They were the sons of a princess and the war god, Mars.

● **As babies, the twin boys** were cast out by their evil great-uncle, who had stolen the king's crown from their grandfather. They survived because a she-wolf found them and let them drink her milk. A bird fed them by putting crumbs in their mouths.

● **When the twins grew** up they overthrew their wicked uncle, restoring their father to his rightful throne.

● **The twins built a new city** on the spot where they had been rescued

by the she-wolf. However, they quarrelled about who should be ruler, and Romulus killed Remus.

● **Romulus became king** of the new city and named it Rome, after himself.

● **The new city had too many men** and not enough women. Romulus hatched a plot whereby he held a great celebration and invited neighbouring communities – then captured all their women!

● **Romulus built an army**, to defend Rome from attacks by local tribes. He brought a 40-year period of peace.

● **One day, Romulus was surrounded** by a storm cloud and taken up to heaven, where he became a god.

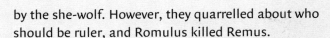

◀ *The Roman legend of Romulus and Remus may have been the inspiration for the Tarzan story. In both cases, abandoned infants were brought up by animals.*

Beowulf

- **The epic poem** *Beowulf* was written in the Anglo-Saxon language by an unknown English person around AD700–750.

- **The legend focuses on the adventures** of a Viking hero, Beowulf. The action takes place in the south of Sweden and Denmark.

- **Christianity came to England** around AD600. The poem blends traditional elements of Norse myth and fate with belief in a Christian god.

- **Beowulf risks his life** to help others by battling three monsters: Grendel, Grendel's mother, and a dragon.

- **The monster Grendel** is said to bear 'the mark of Cain'. This is a reference to the Bible story in which Adam's son Cain killed his brother Abel.

- **Beowulf is fatally wounded** when his warriors desert him – except for his courageous nephew Wiglaf.

▼ *Beowulf has to descend to the depths of a murky lake to fight the monster Grendel's ferocious mother.*

- **At the end of the poem**, the dead Beowulf is laid to rest in a huge burial mound. A similar burial mound, dating around AD650, was discovered at Sutton Hoo in Suffolk in 1939.

- **The oldest manuscript** of Beowulf that exists today was made from an original by monks in about AD1000. Many other older copies were destroyed when King Henry VIII ordered monasteries and their libraries to be closed down in the late 1530s.

- **The modern-day film** *The Thirteenth Knight*, starring Antonio Banderas, is based on the gripping Beowulf legend.

- **The only remaining copy** is kept in a controlled environment behind glass in the British Museum.

Sigurd the Volsung

◄ *J R R Tolkien's Lord of the Rings saga, inspired by the Sigurd legend, has recently been made into three stunning movies.*

- **Different versions of the legend** of the warrior hero Sigurd the Volsung exist in Norse, British and German mythologies.

- **The earliest existing written** version appears as part of the Norse epic poem, *Beowulf*, where a storyteller recites the saga for some warrior nobles.

- **The most detailed** version of the myth is known as *The Volsunga Saga* (written around AD1300 by an unknown author).

- **The legend is a superb adventure** story about heroic deeds, magic, love, betrayal, jealousy, danger and death.

- **Volsung is the King of Hunland**, and great-grandson of the Norse father of the gods, Odin.

- **Volsung's son, Sigmund**, is similarly mighty. He is the only man who can pull Odin's sword out of an oak tree trunk.

- **Odin's favourite is Sigmund's son**, the hero Sigurd. Odin helps Sigurd choose a horse that is related to his own magical steed.

- **Odin's sword was smashed** when Sigmund died. Sigurd has the fragments recast into a fearsome weapon called Gram.

- **Sigurd's first quest is to find** a hoard of dwarf gold, guarded by a dragon. One of the treasures is a cursed ring (inspiration for Tolkien's *Lord of the Rings* saga).

★ STAR FACT ★
The saga contains an early version of the story of *Beauty and the Beast*.

King Arthur

- **Legends about British King Arthur** have been popular for over 800 years, yet historians have never been able to prove whether he was a real figure in history.

- **If a real Arthur did exist**, he is likely to have lived much earlier than the medieval times of the legends.

- **Many authors have written** Arthurian legends, including the French medieval poet Chretien de Troyes and the Victorian poet Lord Tennyson.

- **Arthur's father was said** to be King Uther Pendragon. The name means 'dragon's head'.

- **One legend says Arthur** slew a giant at Mont-Saint-Michel, France, then conquered the Roman Empire.

- **Many legends focus on the knights** at Arthur's court and the idea of courtly love, in which women are purer beings in God's eyes than men.

- **Arthur's knights went on many** dangerous quests to test their bravery and honour. The most difficult was a search for the Holy Grail – a goblet that caught Jesus's blood as he died on the cross.

- **The Round Table** was first mentioned in legends written by the French medieval poet, Robert Wace, in AD1155.

- **Arthur is finally killed** by his enemy Mordred – who is in fact his own son.

- **Some legends say that King Arthur** was taken to a country of blessed souls called Avalon and will return when Britain falls into greatest danger.

◀ Mont-Saint-Michel is a rocky islet off the coast of northwest France, where legend says King Arthur once slew a giant.

Cuchulain

- **Correct pronounciation of** Cuchulain is 'Cu-hoo-lin'.

- **Cuchulain was a warrior hero** supposed to have lived in Ireland in the first century AD.

- **Stories say that Cuchulain was born** when the king of Ulster's sister was magically swept away by a god called Lug. However, the baby's name was originally Setanta.

- **Setanta was schooled by the greatest heroes** and poets at the king of Ulster's court.

- **As a teenager, Setanta killed single-handed a ferocious dog** belonging to a blacksmith called Culan. This is how he got his nickname, because Cuchulain means 'Hound of Culan'.

- **Cathbad the Druid prophesied** that any boy who became a warrior that day would become the most famous hero in Ireland – but would die young. Cuchulain was 15, and decided he wanted a short, glorious life rather than a longer, unremarkable one.

- **Cuchulain was a rare thing called a 'berserk warrior'.** This means he was possessed in battle. Power sparked from his hair, his body hissed with heat, his eyes bulged and blood frothed on his lips.

- **Cuchulain won his wife**, Emer, by defeating the tricks of a cunning chieftain called Forgal the Wily.

- **Cuchulain had been terribly wounded in battle**, but lashed himself to a standing stone, so he would die on his feet, fighting to the end.

- **Cathbad the Druid's prediction came true.** In Irish mythology, Cuchulain is considered to be the greatest of all Irish warrior heroes.

▶ The Celts believed that a goddess of death called Badb often appeared at battlefields in the form of a raven. According to one legend, a raven drank from the wounded Cuchulain's streaming blood as he fought heroically to his death.

Finn McCool

- **The legend of Finn McCool** might be based on a warrior hero living in Ireland in the third century AD.

- **Finn's real name was Demna**. 'Finn' was a nickname meaning 'fair haired'.

- **Finn was raised in secret** by a druidess and a wise woman, who taught him god-like powers.

- **Finn was very wise and just**. This is because he once ate a magical fish called the Salmon of Knowledge.

- **Finn won the position of head** of the Fianna – an elite group of warriors sworn to defend the High King of Ireland. Under Fianna's leadership had many magical adventures and rose to the height of their glory.

- **The Fianna possessed** a magic Treasure Bag which contained weapons from the gods, objects with healing powers, and Faery gifts.

- **Finn fell in love with a goddess**, Sava. She bore him a son, Oisin, who became a famous Fianna warrior and a great poet.

▼ *Legend says that the hero Finn McCool created the rock formation called the Giants' Causeway in Northern Ireland. In fact, it was formed when lava from a volcano cooled and set.*

- **Finn once had an argument** with a giant in Scotland. They threw rocks across the sea at one another, which created a rock formation today called the Giants' Causeway.

- **Legend says that Finn** and the Fianna lived on the Hill of Allen in present-day County Kildare.

- **Finn McCool had a magical 'tooth of knowledge'** that had an extraordinary power, telling him whatever he wanted to know.

Kotan Utunnai

- **The epic poem** *Kotan Utunnai* belongs to a race of people from the Stone Age called the Ainu.

- **The Ainu lived on** remote Japanese islands, untouched by the outside world for hundreds of years, until other Japanese people made contact in around AD1670.

- **The Ainu were hunter-gatherers** who had no agricultural systems, no metalworking skills and no system of writing.

- **The epic** *Kotan Utunnai* was first written down by an English missionary in the 1880s.

- *Kotan Utunnai* is one of several Ainu epic poems which focus on wars with a people called the Okhotsk from the tenth to the sixteenth centuries.

- **Like many epic heroes**, the hero of *Kotan Utunnai* puts family loyalty above his own desires. This means he has to seek revenge for the murder of his parents.

◄ *This is an Attush coat worn by the earliest people in Japan, the Ainu. The patterns around all the openings of the coat are designed to stop evil spirits from entering.*

- **In the myth, the world** of humans is mixed up with the magical world of gods, spirits and demons. Sometimes humans hear the sound of gods fighting – a low rumbling across the land.

- **Many human epic heroes** have god-like qualities, but the hero of *Kotan Utunnai* is so god-like that even the gods themselves sometimes find it hard to believe he is human!

- **Unlike many other epics**, there are several powerful female characters in *Kotan Utunnai*. Women have great fighting skill and are considered equal in importance with men.

- **The epic demonstrates** the Ainu belief that when you die, if you have led a good life you will be reborn. If a wrong-doer, you remain dead.

The Ramayana

- **The Indian epic poem** the *Ramayana* focuses on the battle between the forces of good and evil in the universe.

- **Historians believe that it was** largely composed between 200BC and AD200. The poet is believed to be called Valmiki, although hardly anything is known about him.

- **Like the Greek epic** *The Iliad,* the *Ramayana* involves the rescue of a stolen queen (called Sita).

- **Like the Greek epic** *The Odyssey,* the *Ramayana* follows a hero (Prince Rama) on a long and difficult journey.

- **Prince Rama's enemy** is the mighty demon, Ravana. He can work powerful magic, but is not immortal and can be killed.

- **The demon Ravana's followers** are known as Rakshasas. They can shape-shift and disguise themselves so they do not appear evil. This way, they can tempt good people to do the wrong thing.

- **The poem** demonstrates that it is important to respect animals. Rama needs the help of the hero Hanuman and his army of monkeys to rescue Sita.

- **The story says** that Rama and Sita are earthly forms of the great god Vishnu and his wife, Lakshmi.

- **Hindus see** the *Ramayana* as a book of religious teaching because Rama and Sita are models of good behaviour.

- **The legend ends** when Rama has ruled as king for 10,000 years and is taken up to heaven with his brothers.

▶ *Hindus believe that the hero Rama was one of the ten human forms of the god Vishnu.*

Gassire's Lute

- **An African tribe called the Soninke** have an epic poem called *Gassire's Lute.* It was composed between AD300 and AD1100 as part of a group of songs called the Dausi.

- **Most other songs in the Dausi** have been forgotten.

- *Gassire's Lute* **is a tale** about the ancestors of the Soninke, a tribe of warrior horsemen called the Fasa.

- **The Fasa lived around** 500BC in a fertile area of Africa bordered by the Sahara Desert, Senegal, Sudan and the river Nile.

- **The hero of the legend,** Gassire, is a Fasa prince who longs for his father to die so he can become a famous king.

- **The heroes of other epic poems** usually put their lives at risk trying to help other people. This epic is strikingly different, because the hero puts his own desires in front of everything else.

- **Gassire realizes that all things die,** and that the only way to win lasting fame is to be remembered as a hero in battle songs.

- **Gassire has a lute made,** so he can sing of his own adventures. However, the lute will only play once it has been soaked with blood in battle.

- **Gassire leads his eight sons** and followers into war against an enemy tribe. It is only when all but one of Gassire's sons have been killed that his lute finally sings.

- **Gassire grieves for the dead,** but is filled with joy now he has a great battle song to bring him fame.

◀ *A musician plays a lute by plucking its strings, similar to playing the guitar.*

Mwindo

- **The epic of** *Mwindo* belongs to the Nyanga tribe of Zaire, in Africa.

  - **The poem was first written down** in 1956, when the Nyanga tribe still lived by hunting, gathering and growing their food.

    - **The poem was performed** as a ritual over 12 days to give protection from sickness and death.

      - **The legend begins** when Chief Shemwindo forbids his wives to bear him any male children. Despite this, a little boy is finally born – Mwindo, which means 'first-born male'.

◄ *Storytelling has been a traditional method of keeping myths and legends alive in all cultures.*

- **Shemwindo tries to kill** his son by burying him alive, then by drowning him. Baby Mwindo has superhuman powers which help him escape.

- **Mwindo overcomes his enemies** with the help of friends who include Hedgehog, Spider and Lightning.

- **Mwindo holds a magic sceptre** that he uses to perform powerful spells, such as bringing the dead back to life. He also has a magical bag of good fortune.

- **Mwindo is an example** of good behaviour. He forgives his father and makes peace. In turn, his father makes amends by sharing half of his kingdom with his son.

- **When Mwindo kills** a dragon, Lightning teaches him the lesson that humans are just a part of the universe, not the most powerful thing in it.

- **The main message of the myth** is that all forms of life should have respect for each other: the gods and creation, humans and animals, men and women, the young and the old, the healthy and the sick.

Magical creatures

- **According to Chinese myth** there were five types of dragon: dragons who guarded gods, dragons who guarded emperors, dragons who controlled wind and rain, dragons which deepened rivers and seas, and dragons who guarded hidden treasure.

- **In Greek myth, a centaur** was half-man, half-horse. A satyr was half-man, half-goat.

- **The Phoenix was a magical bird** which lived for 500 years. It died by setting fire to itself, and was then born again from the ashes.

- **Sleipnir was an eight-legged horse** faster than the wind. He belonged to the chief Norse god, Odin.

▶ *Dragons are found in mythologies from all over the world, but play a particularly important role in traditional tales from China.*

- **In 1842 in America**, the famous Phineas T Barnum's travelling circus show displayed a 'real' mermaid. It turned out to be created from a monkey's body and a fish's tail!

- **In the Caribbean**, mermaids are called water-mamas. People believe that if you get hold of a water-mama's comb, she will grant you a wish.

- **Philippine myths** tell of Alan – creatures who are half-human, half-bird. They live in forests and look after children who have lost their parents.

- **Unicorns are featured in the myths** of many civilizations. They are rare, beautiful creatures with the body of a horse and a single, spiral horn.

- **In Chinese mythology**, Hsigo are monkeys with bird-like wings.

- **In myths, salamanders** can survive in fire. Unfortunately, real salamanders are not magically fireproof.

Mythological monsters

- **Myths from the Aborigines** of Australia tell of a swamp monster called the Bunyip who hunts children at night.

- **In Greek mythology**, the Sphinx had a woman's face, a lion's body, and a bird's wings. It killed travellers who could not work out its riddles.

- **Many Scandinavian myths** feature hairy, cruel creatures called trolls who live inside the Earth and are expert metalworkers.

- **Greek stories said that a manticore** had a lion's body, but a human face – with three rows of teeth. It shot poisoned spines from its tail.

- **The Hound of the Baskervilles** was a monstrous dog in a book by the Victorian writer Sir Arthur Conan Doyle. The tale of the gigantic hound from hell has become a modern myth.

- **The Norse hero Beowulf** battled a monster called Grendel. This man-eating hulk is described as a 'shadow-walker' from hell.

- **In Greek myth**, the Chimaera was a fire-breathing monster with a lion's head, a goat's body and a serpent's tail.

- **A gryphon** was a cross between a lion and an eagle, which first appeared in myths of the Middle East.

- **A basilisk or cockatrice** appears in the Bible, as well as Greek legend. It was a snake with a cockerel's wings and a dragon's tail. J K Rowling featured the monster in a Harry Potter story.

- **Medusa the Gorgon** was a female monster in Greek myth who had writhing snakes for hair. Anyone who looked at her face was turned to stone.

◀ *The most famous Sphinx statue in Egypt lies at the foot of Khafre's pyramid at Giza. It would originally have looked like this.*

Modern monsters

◀ *King Kong is a classic US movie made in 1933. It featured a colossal giant gorilla.*

- **There have been thousands** of sightings of a huge sea monster in Loch Ness, Scotland, since it was first reported in AD565.

- **Strange footprints** have been found in West Africa. Stories say they belong to a dinosaur-like swamp creature called the Mokele-Mbende.

- **A huge ape-man nicknamed Bigfoot** or Sasquatch has been seen in North American forests. Two men claimed to have filmed it in 1967, but many believe the film is fake.

- **Since 1983 there have been over 600 sightings** of a big cat similar to a puma on Bodmin Moor, Cornwall – but no firm evidence that such a creature is at large.

- **The Komodo dragon** is a type of giant lizard which lives today in islands in Indonesia.

- **In 1921, the first explorers of Mount Everest** claimed to have seen 'abominable snowmen' or 'Yetis'. There have been many sightings since.

- **The life story of an Englishman** called Joseph Merrick (1862–1890) gave rise to the legend of the Elephant Man. Joseph suffered from Proteus Syndrome which made him horribly disfigured.

- **Myths about werewolves** may have arisen from the illness lycanthropy. Sufferers think they are wild beasts – especially at full moon.

- **Scandinavian stories of gigantic sea monsters** called kraken may be based on real-life giant squid. These are known to have reached out and torn sailors from rafts.

- **The modern myths of Godzilla** and King Kong arose from ideas that giant-sized prehistoric creatures might rise from hiding places and attack civilization.

Giants

- **The Ancient Greeks** believed that the immortals Gaea and Uranus gave birth to three one-eyed giants called the Cyclopes and 300-handed giants called the Hecatoncheires.

- **A giant man holding a club**, carved into the hillside at Cerne Abbas in England, possibly dates from AD185.

- **According to the legends of European settlers** in North America, the Grand Canyon was formed when a giant lumberjack called Paul Bunyan walked along trailing his pickaxe on the ground behind him.

- **In Celtic legend, the Formorian giant**, Balor, had an 'evil eye'. One glance killed whoever it fell upon.

- **In Norse mythology**, giants were the sworn enemies of the gods. Their ruler was King Utgard-Loki.

- **Several passages from the Old Testament** of the Bible tell of tribes and kingdoms of giant-sized people.

- **The most famous giant** in the Bible was the warrior Goliath, killed by the shepherd boy David.

- **In the Mesopotamian** epic poem *Gilgamesh*, the home of the gods in the Cedar Forest of Lebanon was guarded by a giant called Humbaba.

- **In Greek myth**, Talos was a fearsome giant made of bronze who guarded the island of Crete.

- **The tallest man on record** was an American, Robert Wadlow (d.1940). At 2.7 metres tall, he was not as tall as the giants of myths and legends.

► *The Bible story about the giant, Goliath, can be found in the Book of Samuel, Chapter 1 Verse 17.*

Magical possessions

- **The Chinese spirit**, Monkey, had a deadly iron fighting stick which could change magically into a tiny needle, for keeping behind his ear.

- **King Arthur wielded a mighty sword called Excalibur**, given to him by a spirit called the Lady of the Lake.

- **The mighty Norse thunder god, Thor,** had a throwing hammer, Mjollnir, which never missed its target, and a belt, Meginjardir, which doubled his already superhuman strength.

- **The Celtic hero Lug had a boat called Wave-Sweeper** that could travel over land and sea, and a sword called the Answerer that could cut through anything.

- **According to Bible stories**, the prophet Moses had a staff which God enabled to work magic.

- **In the Ramayana, Prince Rama possessed** the god Vishnu's bow, Brahma's shining arrows, and Indra's quiver to keep them in.

◄ *When King Arthur was dying, he ordered Sir Bedivere to throw Excalibur back into the lake it came from. A mysterious hand rose from the waters to claim it.*

- **The Norse goddess** Freya owned a dwarf-crafted necklace, the Brisingamen and also a feather-coat which gave the wearer the power of flight.

- **A Chinese legend tells** how some kind villagers helped the hero Bao Chu by using their own clothes to make him a magic coat. It kept him warm even when he fell into a river of ice.

- **The Dagda, chief of a race of Celtic gods** called the Tuatha De Danann, had a magic cauldron which never ran out of food.

- **Greek myth** says that the god of the Underworld, Hades, owned a helmet of invisibility.

Norse world order

- **Two main written sources** tell us what the Norse people believed about the universe. *The Prose Edda* is a collection of myths recorded by an Icelander called Snorri Sturluson (1179–1241). *The Poetic Edda* is a collection of 34 ancient poems recorded in the seventeenth century.

- **Many Viking carvings show pictures** of what the Norse people believed the universe to be like.

- **The Norse people thought** there were nine worlds arranged on three levels.

- **The uppermost worlds** were: Alfheim – home of the light elves; Vanaheim – home of the fertility gods; Asgard – home of the warrior gods.

- **The middle worlds** were: Midgard – home of humans; Nidavellir – home of the dwarves; Jotunheim – home of the giants; Svartalfheim – home of the dark elves.

- **Norse myth said that a giant serpent** called Jormungand lived in the sea surrounding the middle worlds, circling them.

- **The underworlds** were: Muspellheim – a land of fire; and the freezing land of Niflheim, which included Hel – home of the dead.

▶ *Norse kings had court poets who composed gripping poems about heroes and their battles. The poets performed them on long, cold winter nights as entertainment.*

- **The Norse warrior gods** kept young and strong by eating the Golden Apples of Youth belonging to a goddess called Iduna. Without these, they would face old age and death.

- **Characters from the Norse worlds** such as giants, dwarves and elves also found their way into many European fairy tales.

▶ *According to Norse myth, at the end of the world the giant sea-serpent Jormungand will swim ashore to join a battle against the warrior gods.*

★ STAR FACT ★
Inspiration for the names in J R R Tolkien's
Lord of the Rings trilogy came from characters
in the nine Norse worlds.

Animals and birds

- **According to the Dogon** of Africa, animals once lived in heaven with the Creator. Humans stole a male and a female animal by sliding them down the rainbow.

- **Ravens have lived** at the Tower of London in England for over 1000 years. Myth says that if the birds ever leave, disaster will follow.

- **Stories brought by African slaves** to the Caribbean tell how animals and birds and humans all used to live together, speaking the same language.

- **Ancient Arab legends told** of a big bird called the roc. Modern scientists have found the bones of a giant-sized bird in the swamps of Madagascar.

◀ *A mummified cat and dog from Ancient Egypt. The Ancient Egyptians believed that if they preserved a dead body from decay, its spirit could live for ever.*

- **In Ancient Egypt**, cats were sacred to the goddess Bastet. When a pet cat died, the family had it mummified just like a dead human!

- **The chief Norse god** Odin had two pet ravens, Hugin and Munin. They flew through the universe and brought back news.

- **Around 600BC**, a Greek slave called Aesop collected animal stories which had a moral message. They have become known as *Aesop's Fables*.

- **The Arikara tribe of Native Americans** believed dogs were spirit messengers between them and their gods.

- **Rudyard Kipling's** *Just So* stories (1902) are like myths. They explain how animals came to be as they are – such as how the elephant got his trunk.

- **The Greek goddess** Athena was often pictured with an owl on her shoulder. She was the goddess of intelligence, which is why owls have traditionally been thought of as wise birds.

Natural phenomena

◀ *The glowing lights of the Aurora Borealis can sometimes be seen in the night skies over northern countries such as Norway, Sweden and Iceland.*

- **In Greek myth**, winter occurs because the harvest goddess, Demeter, grieves for six months each year when her daughter, Persephone, has to live in the Underworld.

- **Hawaiian legends say** that the bad-tempered goddess Pele lives inside the volcano Mount Kilauea.

- **In Mayan mythology**, Kisin is an evil earthquake spirit. He lives under the earth with the souls of people who have killed themselves.

- **Many ancient civilizations** have myths which feature 'firebirds', such as the phoenix. These may have arisen from the winged shape of light that blazes around the sun during a total eclipse.

- **Stories from Zambia and Zimbabwe** say a shooting star is the storm god Leza, watching over people.

- **According to the Kono people of Sierra Leone**, the creator god once gave a bat a basket of darkness to look after. The bat spilled some, which is why he flies at night – trying to catch it.

- **Some Native American myths** say that storms are created by an enormous flying creature with flashing eyes called the Thunderbird.

- **In Chinese**, the word 'dragon' also describes thunder and lightning. And tornadoes over oceans are known as 'sea dragons'.

- **According to Norse myth**, the Aurora Borealis, or Northern Lights, are the glowing beauty of a frost giantess called Gerda.

- **An Afro-Caribbean story says** Anansi the spider-man smashed a pot containing all the world's common sense. The wind scattered it – all creatures got some.

Stories of the stars

▶ *Halley's Comet can be seen once every 75 or 76 years. It is featured on the eleventh-century Bayeux tapestry, which shows the conquest of England by the Normans.*

- **Western names for star constellations** come from Classical mythology, such as Orion – the hunter son of sea god Poseidon.

- **Norse myth says** that the stars were sparks that flew out of the firey land of Muspellheim, set in the sky by the gods.

- **According to European settlers in North America**, when Halley's Comet came towards Earth in 1835, Davy Crockett hurled it safely back into space.

- **An ancient myth from the Dogon people** of West Africa tells of a tiny planet that orbits the star Sirius. It was not found by Western scientists until 1862.

- **In Greek mythology**, Antiope was the mother of the evening and morning star.

- **The Bororo tribe of South America believe** that the stars are naughty children who climbed into the heavens to escape punishment, but became trapped.

- **In Inuit legend**, the Pleiades are a pack of hunting dogs who chased Nanook the Bear up into the sky.

- **Astronomy was advanced** in the Toltec, Aztec, Inca and Maya civilizations. The Maya calendar did not just mark a yearly cycle of days and months, but tracked patterns in time over three million years!

- **In Native American mythology**, a hero called Poia who grew up with the Blackfoot tribe was the son of a star and a mortal woman.

- **Some historians think the Ancient Eygptians** built their pyramids to launch the souls of their pharaohs to particular stars, such as the three pyramids at Giza line up with certain stars in the constellation Orion.

Stories of the Sun

- **The Inuit believe** that they lived in total darkness, until Raven flew to a far-off country and stole them a piece of sunlight.

- **A Chinese myth** tells that there were once ten suns who took it in turns to cross the sky. One day they all decided to appear together. The earth began to scorch, so the gods commanded an archer called Yi to shoot dead all but one.

- **The Incas sacrificed** honoured young girls to the sun god, Inti, at the June solstice (the shortest day of the year).

- **An important centre for the worship of Ra-Atum** was Heliopolis. This is Greek for 'sun city'.

▲ *The Sun has been worshipped in many cultures through time.*

- **The Ancient Egyptians** believed that every day the sun god Ra-Atum sailed across the sky in a Boat of Millions of Years. At night, he made a perilous journey through the Underworld.

- **Many Native American plains** tribes held a yearly sun dance that lasted around four days. The dancers aimed to draw the Sun's power into themselves.

- **Navajo Native Americans** believed that a god called Tsohanoai carried the Sun on his back during the day. At night, he hung it on the wall of his house.

- **An Indian myth** tells how the sun god, Surya, was so bright that his wife ran away to live in a shady forest.

- **Myth says that one grandson of the sun goddess** Amaterasu married the goddess of Mount Fuji, and one of their great-grandchildren became Japan's first emperor.

- **The Greek sun god Apollo** was also god of prophecy, music, archery, healing, and protector of shepherds.

Mountains and the Moon

- **Ancient Greeks believed** that Mount Olympus was the home of the gods. It is in northern Greece and is 2917 metres high.

- **The moon god** of the Inuit Native Americans is called Igaluk. They believe he has powers over hunting.

- **According to the Dakota Native Americans**, Hokewingla is a turtle spirit who lives in the Moon.

- **A Chinese myth** said that the Earth was square, and the heavens were supported above it by five mountains (one in each corner and one in the centre). The western mountain, K'un Lun, was the source of the Yellow River.

- **According to Finish mythology**, silver forms in the earth wherever light lands from the Moon, Kuu.

- **Babylonian myth says** that the sun god Shamash drove his chariot every evening to a mighty mountain and disappeared inside.

- **The Greek goddess of the Moon**, Selene, used magic to make a handsome shepherd called Endymion sleep for ever, so she could enjoy his beauty for eternity.

- **Before Mount Everest was renamed** after a western climber (Sir George Everest), its traditional name was Chomo-Lung Ma, which means 'Goddess Mother of the Universe'.

- **According to a Japanese myth**, the moon god, Tsukiyomi, once severely annoyed his sister the sun goddess, Amaterasu. This is why the Sun and the Moon never look each other in the face.

- **The capital city of the Inca Empire**, Machu Picchu, lies up a mountain in the Andes in Peru. At the top of the neighbouring mountain, Huayna Picchu, is an Inca temple to the Moon.

◄ Machu Picchu, capital city of the Inca Empire, was built on a mountain more than 2280 metres above sea-level. This is almost twice as high as the highest mountain in Britain, Ben Nevis.

Rivers, lakes and the sea

- **German legend says** that beautiful mermaids called Lorelei lived on rocks in the river Rhine, luring fishermen to their deaths.

- **In Greek myth**, a Triton is a sea creature like a merman who can control the waves.

- **Norse mythology says that the goddess of the sea**, Ran, owned a huge fishing net to catch sailors.

- **Scottish legends tell of kelpies** – watery ghosts of rivers and lakes.

- **Irish legend** says that the hero Finn McCool slew a phantom and a serpent in Loch Ree. In 1960, three Dublin priests fishing on Loch Ree watched a long-necked monster move through the waters for two minutes.

◀ *The Irish hero Finn McCool accomplished feats of amazing strength and bravery.*

- **Greek myth says that the Aegean Sea** is named after King Aegeus, who drowned himself in the ocean when he believed that his son, Theseus, had been killed.

- **According to Hindu myth**, the goddess Ganga lived in heaven until there was a terrible drought on Earth. Then the god Shiva helped her flow safely down into the world as the sacred river Ganges.

- **A Finnish myth says** that the goddess of the sea and creation, Luonnotar, was once pregnant for 730 years. She gave birth to a man, Vainamoinen. He swam ashore to the country that was to become Finland.

- **A Persian myth tells of a hero called Keresaspa**, who battled for nine days and nights in an ocean with a monster called Gandarewa, who could swallow 12 people at once.

- **The sacred animal of the Greek sea god Poseidon** was the horse. This is perhaps why waves are sometimes described as white horses.

Women

- **According to legend**, the queen of Sheba was a wealthy ruler who lived in modern-day Yemen around 900BC and took a splendid entourage to visit King Solomon of Jerusalem.

- **In Classical myth**, the Amazons were a race of female warriors who lived at the ends of the Earth.

- **The Victorian writer Tennyson** wrote a mythical poem called *The Lady of Shalott* about a woman who chose to break a curse that was upon her – even though it meant she would die.

- **Pocahontas** was a Native American born around 1595. She encouraged peace between the tribes and European settlers, and became a legend .

- **Martha Cannary**, born in Missouri on 1 May 1852, braved many dangerous adventures in the 'Wild West' and became famous as the 'cowgirl', Calamity Jane.

- **According to the Bible**, Mary Magdalene was Jesus's closest female friend.

◀ *The Lady of Shalott was imprisoned in a tower. She was allowed to look at the outside world only via a mirror. If she looked directly through a window, she was cursed to die.*

- **Boudicca** was a legendary queen of the Iceni tribe of Britain, from around AD25 to 61. She raised southeast England in revolt against the Romans.

- **Semiramis** was a mythical queen of Assyria who ruled Babylon, Egypt and Libya for 42 years before ascending to heaven as a dove.

- **In Greek myth** Arachne challenged the goddess Athena to a weaving contest. Athena turned her into a spider!

- **A heroic legend** tells of Violette Szabo, an undercover agent in German-occupied France during World War II. She was captured, imprisoned, tortured and executed.

Holy people and prophets

◀ *The Dome of the Rock is a mosque in Jerusalem built between AD685 and 691 by an Arab caliph.*

- **Legend says that the founder of Sikhism**, Guru Nanak, once disappeared into a river. Days later he emerged, saying that he had been with God.

- **According to Greek myth**, the god Apollo condemned a woman called Cassandra to the fate of prophesying truthfully, but never being believed.

- **Legend says that around AD550 an Indian priest** called Bodhidharma crossed the sea from China to Japan standing on a bamboo. He introduced Zen Buddhism to Japan.

- **The Druid High Priest Cathbad** was a great prophet in Celtic legend.

- **In sixteenth-century France**, Nostradamus wrote prophecies predicting world events as far ahead as AD3500.

- **The earliest prophet of any world religion** was Zoroaster, who was born in northeast Persia (modern-day Iran) around 1200BC.

- **According to Greek myth**, a man called Tiresias was blinded by the gods, but given the gift of prophecy.

- **Mother Shipton was a prophetess** from North Yorkshire, around the sixteenth century. Some people think she predicted the Great Fire of London, railways, aircraft and the Internet.

- **The Dome of the Rock in Jerusalem** was built on the spot from which legend says the Prophet Muhammad ascended into heaven.

- **Some people believe** that all the great holy leaders, including Jesus, Krishna and Buddha, have been manifestations of one great prophet – the Maitreya.

Witches and wizards

- **Stories from eastern Europe** tell of a wicked witch called Baba Yaga. Her house moved on chicken's legs.

- **The magician Merlin** was King Arthur's most trusted advisor. Merlin warned Arthur that Guinevere would bring him grief – and indeed she did.

- **In Sikkim, a tiny kingdom in the Himalayas**, a maharaja died in 1963, Sir Tashi Namgyal. He was believed to be able to control the weather.

- **Greeks and Romans** worshipped the goddess of darkness, Hecate, at crossroads. Today she is worshipped by those who practise black magic.

- **On the Indonesian island of Bali** myths of a witch, Rangda, are acted out. The character came from Queen Mahendradatta who lived 1000 years ago.

- **Aztec sorcerers** used black mirrors of polished obsidian to predict the future. Their patron was the god Tezcatlipoca – 'lord of the smoking mirror'.

- **The story goes** that in the days of Queen Elizabeth I,

all the witches in Hampshire gathered to create a 'cone of power' to chase the Spanish Armada away from England.

- **In 1487**, James Sprenger and Henry Kramer wrote The *Malleus Maleficarum* – a book of rules for detecting witches.

- *Malleus Maleficarum* **was used by the church** in Europe for 300 years to accuse people of black magic .

- **In Greek mythology**, an enchantress called Circe was the aunt of a beautiful witch-girl called Medea. They both knew powerful magic.

▶ *Baba Yaga, a character in eastern European legend, is a typical witch in that she flies through the air on a broomstick and has a talking cat as an assistant.*

Demons and devils

- **'Devil' comes from the Hindu** word 'deva'. 'Demon' comes from the Greek word 'daemon'. The Christian word 'Satan' comes from the Hebrew word 'shatana', which means 'enemy'.

- **Some Nigerian tribes** believe they can drive away demons by summoning up the spirits of their dead ancestors through masked dances.

- **In Japanese mythology,** Oni are demons with two horns, rather like the devils in Christian stories. They wear tiger skins and fly about, hunting for the souls of evil people.

- **In Middle East myths**, fiery demons are often known as 'djin'. They are known in Western myths as 'genies'.

◀ *Stone gargoyles on churches have an important practical function as well as being decorative.*

- **The many demons in Hindu mythology** might have been inspired by the people who lived in India before the ancestors of the Hindus invaded.

- **Gargoyles are carved stone demons** on church roofs. The name comes from a great seventh-century dragon called Gargouille who lived in the river Seine in Paris.

- **The Christian image of the devil** probably came from pictures of the Greek nature god, Pan. Pan was half-man, half-goat, with cloven hooves and two horns.

- **The roofs of Chinese temples** were built curving upwards at the edges so that any demons falling from the sky would be swept up and away.

- **The evil Hindu demon**, Ravana, had ten heads and 20 arms. He tricked the god of creation into giving him special powers of protection, so no god or other demon could harm him.

- **In Sumerian myth,** a dreaded female demon is known as Lamashtu, or 'she who destroys'.

Mysterious places

- **Aborigines** believe that the land is filled with spirits and sacred to their ancestors. Uluru (Ayers Rock) is one of the most holy places.

- **Stonehenge** is a circle of standing stones in Wiltshire, England, dating from around 2800BC.

- **Since the 1980s**, crop circles have been appearing in wheat fields in Britain.

- **Over 200 ships and planes** have vanished in an area off Florida called the Bermuda Triangle. Some believe that strange energies exist here.

- **Many myths have grown up** around a reported UFO crash near Roswell, USA, in 1947. Film footage of aliens has emerged, but never proved to be genuine.

- **At Carnac in France**, thousands of huge stones are arranged in parallel rows.No one knows which ancient people put them there or why.

- **Dozens of giant stone statues** stand on Easter Island in the Pacific Ocean, probably made between AD1000

and 1500. They may represent the guardian spirits of the islanders' ancestors.

- **In 1927,** a pilot discovered enormous line drawings etched into the Nazca plains in Peru. Archaeologists think people created them 1000 to 2500 years ago.

- **Some people believe that the first human moonwalk** in 1969 was a myth made up by USA officials, who were determined to beat the Russians.

- **Varanasi is a city in India** on the banks of the river Ganges. Hindus believe that anyone who washes in the waters will go straight to heaven when they die.

◀ *Uluru, or Ayers Rock, in central Australia is a massive lump of sandstone that rises 335 metres out of the ground.*

Lost locations

- **The Greek writer Plato** described a continent called Atlantis in the Atlantic Ocean, which suddenly vanished. Many have since tried to find its ruins and failed.

- **In the year 2000**, divers discovered the Ancient Greek city of Heraklion at the bottom of the sea near Alexandria.

- **During the sixteenth and seventeenth centuries,** many explorers to South America tried to find a mythical place rich in gold called El Dorado. No one ever found it.

- **In the 1860s,** a French explorer discovered 400 square kilometres of ninth- to thirteenth-century stone temples in the Cambodian jungle. Nearby was the twelfth-century city of Angor Thom, which rivalled Ancient Rome in size and population.

- **Nothing remains of the famous** Hanging Gardens of Babylon (in modern-day Iraq). Stories say that Emperor Nebuchadnezzar built them for his wife, because she missed the hills of her own country, Persia.

- **On 23 August in** AD79, Mount Vesuvius in Italy erupted, burying towns for miles around. More than 1500 years later, the city of Pompeii was discovered, preserved almost perfectly by the lava. Today you can see houses, gardens and even people turned into stone.

▶ *Some scientists think that Vesuvius erupted in pyroclastic flow in* AD79. *Pyroclastic flow is a volcanic avalanche of hot ash, rock fragments and scorching gas which travels at 160 to 240 kilometres an hour.*

- **Off the coast of the Micronesian island** Pohnpei, is the lost city of Nan Madol. It covers 11 square miles of an ancient coral reef and has hundreds of man-made canals and submerged tunnels. It might date from 200BC.

- **In 1845,** the palace of the Assyrian Emperor Sennacherib was discovered in Nineveh – now part of Mosul, Iraq's second largest city.

- **The capital city of the Inca empire**, Machu Picchu, was buried in the Peruvian jungle for centuries until Hiram Bingham stumbled across it in 1911.

- **No one knows if or where King Arthur's city** and castle of Camelot existed. The site was first mentioned by Chretien de Troyes in the twelfth century.

▼ *The lost city of Atlantis might perhaps have been located off the Straits of Gibraltar.*

Mothers and matriarchies

- **Most mythologies** we know of come from male-ruled societies – patriarchies. However, earlier cultures lived in female-ruled societies – matriarchies.

- **Matriarchies** grew from the importance of Mother Earth in producing food and of human mothers in producing children.

- **In many matriarchies**, a young man became the queen's sacred king for a year. He was then sacrificed.

- **The Aztecs** had a terrifying Mother Earth goddess, Coatlicue, who was only satisfied by human sacrifice.

- **Celtic mothers-to-be** used to pray for help in childbirth to the goddess Frigga, Odin's wife.

- **In Greek myth**, the hero Oedipus grew up without knowing his parents. A prophecy said he would unknowingly marry his own mother – it came true!

- **Tlacolteutl was the Aztec goddess of childbirth**, and the mother of the god of maize, Cinteotl, and the goddess of flowers, Xochiquetzal.

- **A great goddess in Ancient Greece** was known by different names including Gaea, Athena, Hera and Aphrodite. When male-dominated myths about Zeus took over, these became less important goddesses.

- **Many Christian stories** tell how the mother of Jesus, Our Lady, has appeared through history in visions to young people.

- **The Hopi**, Hokohan and Zuni Native American tribes lived in a matriarchal society. However, their religious ceremonies were mostly held by men, wearing masks to represent nature spirits.

▶ In the Hopi tribe of Native Americans, women governed their villages and owned all the property, such as the houses.

Trees of life

- **According to Norse myth**, the universe is nine worlds held together in a tree called Yggdrasil.

- **The chief Norse god**, Odin, gained powerful magic by hanging on Yggdrasil for nine days.

- **Early Persians** believed in a tree which grew fruit of immortality, which gave the gods life and strength.

- **The Maya** believed that the universe was laid out in a cross shape, at the centre of which was a life-giving tree.

- **In Mesopotamian myth**, the symbol for the mother goddess Ishtar was a tree of life which looked like a date palm.

- **In Chinese mythology**, the ruler of the eastern sky and his children – ten suns – lived in a palace built in an enormous mulberry tree.

- **Ancient Indians** pressed a mountain plant to produce a sacred liquid, called Soma. This was offered to the gods as a sacrifice.

- **According to the Bacongo people of Zaire**, the god Nzambi created the first intelligent life in the form of a palm tree. This eventually separated into a woman and a man.

- **In Syrian mythology**, Fatima is goddess of the Moon and fate. She is pictured as the Tree of Paradise.

- **The Irish Celts** had a calendar which cited a sacred tree for every month of the year.

▶ According to Norse legend, evil creatures continually tried to destroy the world tree, Yggdrasil, by chewing on its roots, trunk, branches and leaves. A squirrel called Ratatosk scampered up and down every day, carrying messages from top to bottom.

Fertility mythology

- **Farmer's wives in Ancient Greece** often set an extra place at the table hoping that the goddess of the harvest, Demeter, would bless them by joining them at their meal.

- **Each April,** the Aztecs smeared reeds with their blood and offered them to Cinteotl, the god of maize, to ensure a good food supply.

- **The Japanese goddess of fertility and nourishment** for all life was called Uke-Mochi-No-Kami.

- **An Iroquois Native American myth tells** how the corn goddess, Onatah, was kidnapped by the ruler of the Underworld. During the time her mother searched for her, no crops grew. This tale is similar to a Greek myth about the goddess Demeter and her daughter Persephone.

- **In Egyptian mythology,** the fertility goddess Hathor was represented as a cow.

- **According to Slavic legend,** Simargl was a creature like a winged dog. He was responsible for scattering the seeds of every plant across the world.

- **In Sumerian mythology,** Tammuz was god of agriculture. He died each year and was brought back from the Underworld by his lover, Ishtar.

- **The Incas** often sacrificed llamas to a fertility goddess called Pachamama.

- **In Ancient Indian mythology,** the god Indra fights a dragon of drought and releases seven rivers which make the Earth fertile again.

- **Baal** was an important fertility god widely worshipped by ancient peoples in the Middle East.

◀ *According to myth, the cornucopia was the horn of a goat whose milk had fed the god Zeus. It is shown in art overflowing with fruit and vegetables and all the goodness of the harvest.*

Babies and children

- **The Ashanti of Africa** say that a snake taught the first man and woman how to have babies.

- **The Pygmies of Africa** believe that humans were told how to have children by the Moon.

- **The Chaga people of Africa** have a myth in which a mountain spirit turns four gourds into children as company for a sad, lonely widow woman.

- **In Celtic legend,** the Little People or faeries sometimes swap a human baby for a faery one. The faery baby is called a changeling.

- **The Greeks** worshipped Hera as goddess of marriage and childbirth. Her Roman name, Juno, is why it is traditionally lucky to get married in June.

- **Newly married couples in China** pray to a kind goddess called Kwan Yin for help in conceiving a baby.

◀ *The modern-day myth of Santa Claus developed from the story of Saint Nicholas.*

- **Lupercalia was a Roman festival** in which shepherds made goatskin whips and ran through the streets striking anyone they met. Women believed this would make them more likely to bear children!

- **Greek myth** says that when the hero Heracles was a baby, the goddess Hera sent two huge snakes to kill him. Heracles simply strangled them!

- **In Japanese mythology,** Kishi-Bojin is a goddess who protects children.

- **Traditionally, European countries** celebrated the feast of Saint Nicholas on 6 December by giving presents to children. This gradually developed into the myth of Santa Claus.

Tales of beauty

- **In Greek myth**, the goddesses Hera, Athena and Aphrodite wanted to know who was the most beautiful. The chief god, Zeus, asked a Trojan prince called Paris to decide. Paris picked Aphrodite, because she promised him the most beautiful woman in the world.

- **Classical myth says that the most** beautiful woman in the world was Helen, queen of Sparta – the daughter of Zeus and the goddess Nemesis.

- **Paris seized Helen** as his reward and stole her away to Troy. This action caused the start of the Trojan Wars.

- **According to Greek myth**, Aphrodite was goddess of beauty and love. At her birth, she emerged from the sea naked and fully grown, and the winds blew her ashore.

- **The Romans adopted Aphrodite** under the name of Venus. Venus was also the official protector of the Roman people.

- **In Hindu myth**, Lakshmi was the goddess of beauty and good fortune.

- **The Norse goddess of beauty**, Freya, drove a chariot pulled by two large cats.

- **The Celts** had a god of beauty and love – Angus Og.

- **A Celtic story** says that the wizard Math magicked a beautiful wife for the hero Llew Llaw Gyffes out of blossoms. She was named Blodeuwedd, or 'flower face'.

- **The legend of Beauty and the Beast** was first recorded by a French writer called Madame Gabrielle de Villeneuve, in 1740.

◄ This life-sized statue of the goddess Venus (Greek name: Aphrodite) is around 2100 years old. She is called the Venus de Milo, because she was found on the island of Milos in the Aegean Sea during the second century BC.

Stories of strength

▶ The sport of Sumo wrestling began in Japan around 20BC The heaviest Sumo wrestlers weigh 250 kilograms, which is twice as heavy as the heaviest world-champion boxer.

- **The Greek hero Heracles** had superhuman strength from birth.

- **According to Norse myth**, the god Thor once found he was not strong enough to pick up the giant king's cat. It turned out to be the enormous world serpent, Jormungand, disguised by magic.

- **In Japanese legend**, Kintaro ('the golden boy') had amazing strength. In one story, he uprooted a tree and smashed a giant spider over the head with it.

- **Hindus believe that the god Shiva** is the special strengthener of warriors.

- **In Persian myth**, the strength of Mother Earth was given the form of a bull, which roamed the Earth for 3000 years. The god Mithras finally killed it, and its strength went to the gods in the heavens.

- **According to Greek myth**, the Titan Atlas holds the sky on his shoulders.

- **Norse stories say the gods tethered a monster**, Fenris Wolf, with a ribbon called Gleipnir. It was made of dwarf-magic and was stronger than any chain.

- **According to legend, the first Sumo match** took place between the Japanese god Take-mikazuchi and the leader of a rival race, to decide who should live in the Japanese islands.

- **The Bible tells of an Israelite called Samson** who had amazing strength, as long as he did not cut his hair.

- **A modern myth about a warrior princess** called Xena has been created for a TV series. Xena not only has amazing strength, she also knows powerful magic.

Old age and long life

- **In Classical myth**, a prophetess called the Sibyl wished to live for 1000 years. However, she forgot to ask for eternal youth. She gradually aged and shrunk until she had to live in a bottle.

- **In another Classical myth**, the goddess Eos asked Zeus to make her lover Tithonus immortal. She too forgot to ask for eternal youth, and Tithonus became a withered old man for ever.

- **The modern film *Highlander*** created a myth about a race of warriors who only die if their heads are cut off. Many of the warriors live for centuries!

- **The American writer Washington Irving** (1783–1832) wrote a story called *Rip Van Winkle* based on a Dutch legend. Rip nods off in a dwarf cavern and wakes to find that he is 20 years older!

- **A Norse story** tells how a wrinkled old woman called Elli once wrestled the great god Thor to one knee. Elli was Old Age in disguise.

▶ *The story* Rip Van Winkle *was first published in 1820.*

- **The Chinese god, Shou Lao,** decides how long a person will live.

- **In Japanese mythology,** tortoises and storks often symbolize old age.

- **In Celtic legend**, the goddess Niamh carried away an Irish prince called Oisin to the Land of Youth, Tir Nan Og. When Oisin returned home, he had been away for 300 years!

- **In Celtic myth**, Lir was the Old Man of the Sea. His second wife secretly turned his children into swans and drove them away. By the time Lir found them they had become old people.

- **According to the Bible**, in the early days people lived much longer than they do now. Noah lived for 950 years!

Legendary partnerships

◀ *Legend says that the outlaw Robin Hood and his band of Merry Men lived in Sherwood Forest, near Nottingham in England.*

- **Robert Leroy Parker and Harry Longabaugh** were American outlaws who held up banks and trains in the 1890s. They became known in legend as Butch Cassidy and the Sundance Kid.

- **The Norse gods** Thor and Loki once partnered up to win back Thor's magic hammer from a giant who had stolen it. They went to the giant's castle disguised as a bride and bridesmaid!

- **The American legend** of lovers Bonnie Parker and Clyde Barrow tells how they went on a spree of robbery and murder before being shot dead by police in 1934.

- **In Greek myth**, Scylla was a monster who lived in a clifftop cave above a whirlpool called Charybis.

- **In Afro-Caribbean animal legends** written by Uncle Remus, the wily Brer Rabbit always outsmarts his arch-enemy, Brer Fox.

- **A Wild West legend** says that the outlaw Billy the Kid was close friends with a sheriff called Pat Garrett.

- **English legends about a hero** called Robin Hood who teamed up with a gang of Merry Men to rob the rich and give to the poor have been told since the fourteenth century.

- **The legendary superhero Batman** first appeared as a cartoon in detective comics in 1937.

- **According to the Fon people of Africa**, the world remains fertile due to the partnership of Sagbata, god of the earth, and Sogbo, god of the sky.

- **Margot Fonteyn and Rudolph Nureyev** became a legendary ballet dancer partnership in the 1960s.

Learning and knowledge

- **The Celtic goddess of learning was called Brigid.** This means 'the powerful one'.

- **According to Norse myth**, the chief warrior god, Odin, bought a drink from the Fountain of Knowledge at the foot of the World Tree. The price was one of his eyes.

- **In Chinese myth**, Guan Di is the wise god of law, martial arts and diplomacy.

- **Japanese people** believed that it was their god of learning, Tenjin, who taught them how to write.

◀ The Ancient Egyptians used hieroglyphics to write inscriptions on the walls of tombs and temples, and to write religious texts on papyrus scrolls. Only priests and scribes knew how to write.

- **Ancient Egyptians believed that it was their god of wisdom**, Thoth, who had devised laws, worked out how to measure time, and invented hieroglyphics.

- **According to Inca legend**, the creator god Viraccocha roamed the world to teach mankind wisdom, but people were too busy with crime and war to listen.

- **The Maori people of New Zealand** recite their traditional culture of myth in a chant, Wharewananga, meaning 'school of learning'.

- **In Tibetan** Buddhism, eight giant warriors called Dharmapalas have the power to scorch enemies of Truth with the light of perfect knowledge.

- **The Hindu god of learning is Hanuman**, who is half-human, half-monkey.

- **According to Muslim Shia stories**, teachers called Sayyids are direct descendants of the Prophet Muhammad who are gifted with learning from birth.

Living happily ever after

- **In Greek myth**, Penelope was the wife of the hero Ulysses. She waited faithfully for 20 years for her husband to return from the Trojan Wars.

- **The Japanese goddess of love, Benten**, once set out to get rid of an evil Serpent King. However, the couple fell in love!

- **In a Robin Hood myth**, the folk hero rescued Maid Marian from King John I and married her himself.

- **A Chinese myth** tells how a servant once disguised himself as a magical rainbow-coloured dog and won the emperor's permission to marry his daughter.

- **Celtic prophecy said that a girl called Deirdre** would bring ruin on Ireland, so King Conchobar of Ulster hid her away in a castle deep in a forest. She escaped to Scotland with the king's own nephew.

- **According to Roman myth**, Psyche was a girl who boasted that she was more beautiful than the goddess Venus. Venus sent the god Cupid to punish her, but he fell in love with her. They ran away together and Psyche was finally made a goddess.

- **The Greek hero Perseus** rescued Andromeda from sacrifice to a sea monster. They live on as star names.

- **There are many Japanese myths** in which faithful lovers are turned into pine trees – a symbol of fidelity.

- **The Scottish legend Tam Lin** tells of a girl who wins a man held by the queen of Faery by holding him tight as the queen changes him into terrifying creatures.

- **The Indian prince Siddhartha Gautama** (563–483BC) left behind all his riches, and wandered the world until he found the secret of true happiness. He became known as the Buddha.

▶ The Queen of Faery has terrifying magical powers in the Scottish legend of Tam Lin.

Tragic love stories

- **In Greek myth**, Narcissus was a handsome youth who fell in love with his own reflection. He killed himself in despair.

- **Possibly the most famous legendary lovers** are the Roman General, Mark Antony, and the 'enemy' queen of Egypt, Cleopatra, who lived around 40BC Due to the conflict in Antony's loyalties, he committed suicide.

- **According to Aztec myth**, the god of the wind, Ehecatl, fell in love with a mortal called Mayahuel. Unfortunately, his divine lovemaking killed her!

- **The famous ballet** *Giselle* is based on a German legend about a girl who dies of a broken heart.

- **Classical myth says that** Dido, queen of Carthage, killed herself when her Trojan lover, Aeneas, was told by the gods to leave her.

▲ When Queen Cleopatra of Egypt discovered that Antony had committed suicide, she killed herself too. On their deaths, in 30BC, Egypt was taken by the Roman Empire.

- **A South American myth** says that a woman called Cavillaca fled from the passionate advances of the creator god Coniraya. They were both turned into rocks in the sea.

- **The tragic love story of Romeo and Juliet** was not Shakespeare's idea. The tale existed in different forms for thousands of years before the great playwright magically reworked it.

- **One of the earliest** Romeo and Juliet stories was Babylonian. A youth called Pyramus was led to believe that his lover, Thisbe, was dead. He killed himself– but Thisbe was in fact alive and well! In grief, she committed suicide.

- **The love affair between King Arthur's wife**, Guinevere, and his best friend, Sir Lancelot, brought no one happiness. Lancelot was banished and the alliance of the Knights of the Round Table collapsed. The weakened Arthur was killed and the remorseful Guinevere went to live in a convent.

- **Arthurian legend** says that Merlin fell in love with the Lady of the Lake and taught her all the secrets of his sorcery. She repaid the magician by imprisoning him in a glass tower.

◀ The love affair between King Arthur's wife, Guinevere, and his best friend, Sir Lancelot, first entered Arthurian legend in the stories of the French writer Chretien de Troyes in the twelfth century.

Inspiration and courage

- **On 29 September 1914** a story by William Machen appeared in a newspaper about angels helping British soldiers in a World War I battle. Machen later realized he had created a modern myth when he found other versions of his story, all claiming to be true.

- **The legend of Joan of Arc** tells how a peasant girl led the armies of the king of France in the fifteenth century. Burnt as a witch, she was later made a saint.

- **A Swiss legend says that William Tell** was once forced to shoot an arrow at an apple on his son's head – which the hero did safely.

- **Hindus tell legends of Mahatma Ghandi** (1869–1948). A Hindu leader, he led peaceful protests against British rule in India in support of rights for the poorest Indians.

▶ Mahatma Ghandi's real name was Mohandas Ghandi. His followers called him 'the Mahatma' which means 'great soul'.

- **In 1838, lighthouse keeper's daughter Grace Darling** bravely rowed through stormy seas to rescue nine survivors of a shipwreck on the Farne Islands.

- **Classical legend tells how around 2200 years ago,** a brilliant Carthaginian general called Hannibal used elephants to cross the Alps to battle the Romans.

- **The legend of Spartacus** tells the story of an escaped Roman gladiator who from 73–71BC led 120,000 runaway slaves in an uprising for their freedom.

- **In 1297, William Wallace led a Scottish uprising** against the English. Legends tell of the hero's passion for national freedom.

- **The nun Mother Teresa** spent 50 years nursing the sick and dying among the poorest people in Calcutta.

- **The legend of nurse Florence Nightingale** (1820–1910) suggests she was an angelic 'lady with a lamp'. In fact, this pioneering woman was tough, driven and highly organized.

Stories of fire

- **Stories say that the Greek god Zeus** did not want humans to have the secret of fire. A Titan called Prometheus stole fire and gave it to humans.

- **The Kayapo tribes of South America** believe that a jaguar once adopted an abandoned boy called Botoque and taught him the secret of making fire.

- **In Ancient Persian myth,** Atar was the god of fire and defender of creation.

- **In the Persian religion of Zoroastrianism,** fire is the symbol of the creator god, Ahura Mazda. Zoroastrians worship in fire temples.

- **A temple to Vesta,** goddess of fire, stood in the heart of Rome's Forum. A sacred flame burnt continually.

- **The ancient Hindu fire god Agni** was worshipped for his warmth and light, but also feared for his powers of destruction.

- **Hephaestus was blacksmith to the Greek gods.** His fiery furnace was believed to lie under the volcano

Mount Etna in Sicily. The Roman name for Hephaestus was Vulcan.

- **According to Lithuanian myth,** Kalvaitis was a blacksmith god who remade the sun each day and sent it red-hot across the sky.

- **In a South Pacific myth,** the god Maui tricked the goddess Mahui-Ike into giving him the gift of fire. When she realized, she set the whole world ablaze.

- **In Japanese mythology,** when the spirit of fire, Kagutsuchi, was born, he scorched his mother so badly that she died.

▶ According to Hindu belief, the fire god Agni acts as a link between people and the heavens, because the smoke from his sacred flames rises up into the skies. With three heads aflame, he rides on a ram called Vahana.

Friendships with animals

- **In Cherokee and Creek Native American myth**, food was once so scarce that bears offered to be hunted for meat and skins.

- **A Scottish legend tells how a faithful dog**, Bobby, guarded his master's grave in Greyfriars churchyard, Edinburgh, from 1858 until his death 14 years later.

- **According to Roman myth**, if a hedgehog peeped out of its burrow on 2 February and saw a shadow, there would be six more weeks of winter. The American ritual of Groundhog Day is based on a similar belief.

- **A story recorded by a Greek slave called Aesop** tells how a man called Androcles was thrown to the lions.

▶ *The friend of the Inuit people, the bowhead whale, grows to be 15 to 18.5 metres long. Its arched mouth can be up to 3 metres wide and 6 metres deep!*

- However, the lion refused to eat him. Androcles had once pulled a thorn from its injured paw!

- **In 1912**, Edgar Rice Burroughs wrote a book about a child who was brought up by gorillas in the jungle. The legend of Tarzan was born.

- **Christian stories say that Saint Francis of Assisi** communicated with animals, birds and fish, and preached to them just as he did to humans.

- **The legendary hero** the Lone Ranger rode a faithful white horse who was summoned by, 'Hi-yo, Silver!'

- **A Russian myth** tells how a wise grey wolf helps a Tsar's son, Ivan, to search for the legendary firebird.

- **An Inuit myth says that the Supreme Spirit** made the bowhead whale to be their best friend. He allowed the Inuit to hunt the creature for food, skins and tools.

- **In 1956 in Kenya** Joy Adamson adopted a lion cub, Elsa, and trained her to return to the wild. Legend says Joy was killed by a lion (she was murdered).

Eternal life

- **Egyptian gods** are sometimes pictured holding a symbol called an Ankh as though it were a key. This symbolized the opening of the gates of death to immortality.

- **The Ancient Chinese religion**, Taoism, teaches belief in eight immortals who discovered a magical elixir of life which allowed them to live for ever.

- **In Medieval Europe**, early scientists called alchemists strove to create an elixir of life to cure all illnesses.

- **The Celtic god Govannon** is a blacksmith who also brews a mead of eternal life.

- **The mischievous Chinese spirit, Monkey**, was once appointed Guardian of the Garden of Immortal Peaches – but he ate all the heavenly fruit and became immortal himself!

- **In Arabic, 'khuld' means eternal life**. Islamic stories teach that all souls are immortal – some will go to heaven and others will go to hell.

- **In Roman mythology**, Jupiter punished a traitor called Janus by giving him immortality but taking away his freedom to move. Janus was made to stand for ever as Heaven's gatekeeper.

- **Sengen is the Japanese goddess of blossom** and the sacred mountain Fujiyama. She guards the secret Well of Eternal Youth.

- **In Chinese myth**, cranes are used as symbols of immortality.

- **In Greek myth**, ambrosia was the food of the gods. Anyone who ate it became immortal.

▼ *The sacred Mount Fuji is the highest mountain in Japan. In summer, people climb to the Shinto shrine at its summit.*

Health and healing

▲ According to Greek myth, a centaur was a creature with the body and legs of a horse, but the chest, arms and head of a man.

- **The Navajo tribe of Native Americans** made coloured sand pictures of spirits, which they believed had the power to heal.

- **Iroquois Native American myth** tells how a tribe was once dying of illness. The animals prayed to the Supreme Spirit, who showed a brave called Nekumonta a spring of healing waters.

- **Hindu myth tells of a famous doctor** called Yama-Kumar. His father, the Lord of Death, told him whether or not he would be able to heal each of his patients.

- **Medieval myths** said that the Mandrake plant had healing powers, but that when it was pulled out of the ground, it gave a scream which drove people mad.

- **Legend says that the Brazilian Jose Arigo** (1918–1971) had miraculous psychic powers which enabled him to perform thousands of operations such as eye surgery without any medical training or anaesthetic.

▶ Mandrake root is famous for being a chief ingredient in witches' brews. According to legend, it was only safe to pull the plant out of the ground after performing a special chant and ritual in the moonlight.

- **According to Greek myth**, when the sea goddess Thetis had a baby boy by a mortal, she tried to save the child from harm by dipping him in the river Styx. The sacred waters protected the baby everywhere except the one heel she was holding. The child grew up to be the hero Achilles.

- **Asclepius, the Greek god of healing**, was taught the arts of medicine and surgery by a wise centaur called Chiron.

- **In Ancient Persian** myth, the hero Thrita could protect humans from disease and death because his prayers brought forth plants of healing.

- **The Inuit god of healing** was Eeyeekalduk. He was depicted as a tiny old man who lived inside a pebble.

- **The Japanese god of medicine**, Sukuna-Biko, was so small that he could rest on a stalk of millet.

Struggle with fate

- **According to gypsy belief**, there are three female spirits of fate. Two are good, but one seeks to harm humans.

- **Norse myth tells of three women** who decide the fate of humans – the Norns.

- **The Greeks and Romans** also believed in three women who set destiny, called the Fates.

▲ Historians think that Delphi was a sacred site in Greece long before the worship of the god Apollo in ancient times. Female figurines dating back to the twelfth century BC have been found, which indicates that an early earth goddess was worshipped there.

- **The Vikings** believed that even their warrior gods were fated to die one day.

- **Although the Classical gods** and goddesses often helped their favourite mortals, they never tried to change their destined deaths.

- **The Greeks believed that the god Apollo** told what was fated to happen through an oracle at Delphi in Greece.

- **Today in Italy**, you can still see the cave at Cumae where a famous seer called the Sibyl spoke of things fated to happen.

- **The Fon god of fate, Legba**, is shown as an old man leaning on a stick used to prop up the universe.

- **Slavic peoples believed that the spirits of female ancestors** appeared at the cradle of a newborn baby and decided its destiny.

- **The Celts did not fear fate**, as they believed that death was merely a passage from this life to a happy land where everyone lived in eternal bliss.

Warnings and curses

- **Celtic peoples** believed that anyone who heard the wail of a spirit woman called a Banshee would soon die.

- **In Greek myth**, the inventor Daedalus made wings for himself and his son Icarus, to escape from prison. Daedalus warned Icarus not to fly too near to the sun, but Icarus forgot. His wings burned and he plunged to his death in the ocean.

- **According to the Eastern Orthodox Church**, the body of anyone bound by a curse will not decay, so they cannot find peace.

- **In 1798, Coleridge** wrote a poem called *The Rime of the Ancient Mariner* based on an ancient curse: any sailor who shoots an albatross brings doom upon his crew.

- **Medieval legends say the 'Wandering Jew'** was a man who mocked Jesus as he was carrying the cross. Jesus cursed him to walk the Earth till the end of time.

◄ The word 'banshee' comes from the Irish Gaelic 'bean sidhe', which literally means 'woman of the fairy mound'.

- **In English myth**, a Grant looks like a bright prancing horse. Whoever sees it is cursed with bad luck.

- **The Greek god Zeus** cursed a prophet called Phineas for being too truthful to mortals. Whenever Phineas sat down to eat, creatures called Harpies swooped down and snatched his food away.

- **In 387BC, a Roman called Caedicius** heard a voice warning that the city walls should be strengthened. The Roman authorities did not believe him. Not long afterwards, invading armies of Gauls arrived.

- **According to German myth**, if you see your own double (or 'doppelganger') you will soon die.

- **Christians believe that** the Curse of Eve is the pain women suffer during childbirth.

Wrath and punishment

- **Egyptian myth** says that illnesses were brought into the world by the lion-headed goddess Sekhmet to punish humans, who were turning against the sun god, Ra-Atum.

- **A Greek nymph called Echo** once so annoyed Zeus by being a chatterbox that he took away her speech. From then on, she could only repeat the words of others.

- **German legend says that in 1284** a mysterious musician called the Pied Piper rid the town of Hamelin of a plague of rats. When the townspeople refused to pay him, he lured the children away.

- **In Greek myth** an evil king called Tantalus was punished in the Underworld. Chained up near to water and food, when he reached for it, it moved.

- **Hittite myth** says that the world is punished when the bad-tempered fertility god Telepinu is angry, as nothing will then grow.

◀ *This Viking carving shows the Norse trickster Loki. Half-god and half-giant, he was often friendly, fun company for the gods, but turned malicious.*

- **In 1909, 19-year-old Robert Stroud** began a lifetime sentence for manslaughter and other crimes. He spent years studying birds and became known as Birdman of Alcatraz.

- **The Greeks believed** in a goddess responsible for punishing wrong-doers, called Nemesis.

- **In Chinese myth**, Buddha punished the naughty Monkey by making him accompany a young priest from India to bring Buddhist teachings to China.

- **Wicked Norse god Loki** was punished by being bound to a rock in fetters made from his own son's body. A snake was fixed to drip venom on his head for ever.

- **In Greek myth**, Zeus punished the Titan Prometheus for giving humans the secret of fire by nailing him to a mountain and setting an eagle to tear out his liver.

Flood mythology

- **Historians think many flood myths**, including the Bible tale of Noah's Ark, may have arisen from a flood between 3000 and 2000BC in Mesopotamia.

- **The Sumerian poem** *Gilgamesh* tells how the ruler of the gods, Enlil, sent a flood to destroy the world. Utanapishtim built an ark and saved his family and specimens of every animal, bird and plant.

- **Greek myth** tells that Zeus once flooded the world. A man called Deucalion and his wife, Pyrrha, survived by building a boat and filling it with provisions.

- **According to Norse myth**, a flood killed all the Rime Giants except one. The wise Bergelmir survived by building a roofed boat for himself and his family.

- **The Mandan Native Americans** believed that animals once helped a hero build a huge canoe to save their tribe from a terrible flood.

- **A Chinese myth says the thunder god** flooded the world. Only two humans survived, a little boy and girl.

- **According to Guarani and Caribbean flood myths**, the survivors escaped by climbing tall trees.

- **Inca myth says that the sun god** once flooded the world to destroy it, then sent his son, Manco Capac, and his daughter, Mama Ocllo, to the Earth to teach people civilization and proper worship of the Sun.

- **In Borneo myth**, a woman was the sole surivor of a flood which wiped out humans. She mated with the flames of her camp fire and repopulated the world.

- **According to the Tupinamba of South America**, Monan the creator grew fed up with ungrateful humans and destroyed the world by fire. He saved one man, Irin-Mage, who begged Monan to quench the fire with a huge flood and give the world a second chance.

▶ *The Bible story of the Flood says that Noah's Ark came to rest at the top of Mount Ararat, which is in modern-day Turkey.*

Evil and death

- **Many African tribes believe** that death entered the world by mistake. For instance, Burundi myth says that the creator was chasing death out of the world when a woman got in his way, so death escaped to freedom.

- **In Banyarwanda myth**, the creator once hunted Death. He told everything to stay indoors, so Death could not hide. But an old woman went out to hoe her vegetable garden, and Death hid under her skirt and was taken inside.

- **According to Greek myth**, a girl called Pandora opened a forbidden sealed box. It contained every evil and sorrow, and they all flew out into the world.

- **According to some Native American myths**, the god Coyote decided that humans should die. He regretted this bitterly when he could not save his own son from a snake bite.

- **A Caraja myth from South America says that** the first humans lived underground and were immortal. When they discovered the beautiful land above the Earth, many people stayed and lived there, even though they would one day become old and die.

- **According to Norse myth**, a giantess witch called Gullveig once wandered about the world of humans, bringing sin and misery.

- **The Navajo Native Americans** believed that all evils entered the world from the east: sickness, wars and white people.

- **A myth from New Zealand says** that the Dawn-maiden once unknowingly committed a crime and fled to the Underworld. Ever since, she has dragged people down to the land of the dead to be with her.

▶ In the mythologies of many European countries, Death is pictured as being a silent figure in a dark cloak. His hood hides his face – a skull. He sometimes carries a scythe with which he cuts short human lives, and is then called 'the Grim Reaper'.

◀ The myth of Pandora's Box says that evils and sorrows flew into the world like stinging insects. However, the Box also contained a bright-winged butterfly – hope.

- **A Sudanese myth** tells how the mother of a dead child once begged the god Ajok to bring her baby back to life. When the father found out he was horrified, and killed the child again. From then on, Ajok left death as permanent among his people.

- **In Papua New Guinean myth**, Honoyeta was a demon who could take on the form of a human or a snake. One day, one of his wives burnt his snakeskin, so he was stuck in his human form for ever. As retaliation, Honoyeta brought death to humans.

Burial beliefs

- **The Greeks believed that Hades**, god of the Underworld, taught burial practices to mortals, to show respect for the dead.

- **The Bushpeople of Botswana** believe that Gauna (or Death) taught them burial rituals in order to keep ghosts in their graves.

- **Zoroastrians** believe dead bodies are a home for Angra Mainy, the force of evil. They are left out for vultures.

- **In Java,** stories say that anyone who wishes to receive a message from a spirit should spend the night alone in the mortuary.

- **Hindu stories** say that if the ashes of a dead person are scattered on the river Ganges at the holy city of Varanasi, their soul will be nearer to breaking out of a circle of death and rebirth, and so closer to heaven.

- **Arthurian legend** says that Lancelot captured a castle – Dolorous Gard. In it, he found a tomb with his own name on. He was destined to be buried there.

◄ *Vultures and birds called condors feed mainly on dead and dying animals, known as carrion.*

- **In Finnish myth**, the goddess of death and decay, Kalma, is believed to haunt graves, snatching the flesh of the dead.

- **Greeks and Romans** believed a dead body (or its burnt ashes) should be covered with earth – even a symbolic handful. If not, the dead person's soul would not find its way into the Underworld.

- **When the Greek hero, Jason**, was fleeing from the king of Colchis, the witchgirl Medea cut up the king's son (her brother) and scattered the body behind Jason's ship. The pursuing king stopped to collect the pieces in order to give his son a burial, so Jason and his crew of Argonauts escaped.

- **At a Chinese funeral**, mourners burn fake money. This is as an offering to the gods of the Underworld, so they will allow the dead person to pass through and reach heaven.

Legendary 'baddies'

- **The Roman Emperor Caligula** (AD12–41) was an evil tyrant who hated his own people and loved torture.

- **Ghengis Khan, a ruthless military leader**, united the Mongol tribes into an empire around AD1200.

- **The most famous American gangster**, Al Capone, was born in Brooklyn, New York in 1899. He lived a life of crime in Chicago and died in 1947 – from ill health.

- **Edward Teach, better known as Blackbeard**, attacked so many ships in only two years that he became the most famous pirate ever, before being killed in 1718.

- **Anne Bonny and Mary Read** were two women pirates caught on the *Revenge* ship in 1720. They were sentenced to be hanged, but Anne mysteriously disappeared from prison and Mary died of fever.

- **Attila was a savage warrior** who united the Hun tribes of Eastern Europe into a mighty empire in the fifth century. The Romans called him 'the Scourge of God' because of the destruction he wreaked.

- **A story says that in Victorian times** a poor barber, Sweeney Todd, lived in London. He killed his customers and a neighbour made the bodies into pies!

- **Ghede (or Baron Samedi)**, sinister god of the dead in Haitian Voodoo mythology, wears dark glasses and a black tail-coat and top hat, and loves to drink rum!

- **European myth** tells of Faustus who sold his soul to the devil in return for earthly power and riches.

- **In some Jewish and Islamic stories** the first woman God created was not Eve, but Lilith. She ran away from Adam, slept with Satan, and bore demon children.

▼ *Legend says that before battle, Blackbeard braided his whiskers into pigtails and stuck slow burning matches into them so his face was wreathed in smoke.*

Underworlds

- **Classical myth** says that a fearful three-headed dog, Cerberus, guarded the entrance to the Underworld.

- **Ancient Greeks believed** that if a god or goddess swore an oath on an underworld river called the Styx, they were not allowed to break it.

- **The Greeks believed** that another river in the Underworld was called the Lethe. Each spirit drank from it to forget their past life.

- **According to the Ainu of Japan**, all souls go to an underworld called Pokna-Moshiri where the good are rewarded and the bad are punished.

◀ Greek myth tells how the hero Heracles tied up the three-headed hell-hound Cerberus, dragged him to King Eurystheus's court and returned him to the Underworld.

- **In Welsh mythology**, a cauldron of the Underworld is owned by a goddess called Cerridwen. She uses it to brew a mead of divine knowledge and inspiration.

- **The Iroquois Native Americans** believed that forces called Ohdows controlled the Underworld and stopped spirits coming to the surface.

- **Mictlan** is the ninth and lowest level of the Mayan Underworld. It is the cold, dark realm of the wicked.

- **In the mythology of Finland**, the Underworld is called Tuonela. It is a place of diseases and corpse-eating monsters.

- **The queen of the Norse** Underworld was Hela, the goddess of death. She was half-living, half-corpse. She ruled over the spirits of those who did not die in battle.

- **In Libyan mythology**, the Underworld is ruled by the goddess of death and prophecy, Echidne. She is half-woman, half-serpent.

Pictures of paradise

- **The Celts believed** that various 'otherworlds' existed. Tir Nan Og (or Tir inna Beo) was a paradise which looked like Earth, only far more beautiful.

- **According to Celtic myth**, one peaceful refuge for blessed spirits was the enchanted island of Avalon.

- **One Celtic myth** said that a man called Donn, one of their ancestors – the Children of Mil – was buried on a small island off the coast of Ireland. They believed Donn would welcome their spirits to live with him.

- **In some Classical myths**, Elysium is a happy realm at the ends of the earth for heroes. In others, it is a peaceful place in the Underworld where good souls rest before being reborn.

- **According to Norse myth**, warriors who died bravely in battle were taken by female spirits called Valkyries to the gods' home, Asgard. They lived there in a palace called Valhalla.

- **Tillan-Tlapaallan** is one of three Aztec heavens. It is reserved for those who share in the wisdom of the god Quetzalcoatl.

- **According to Fijian myth**, Burotu is an island of eternal life and joy where the souls of good people will go to rest in the cool shade.

- **Islamic stories say that paradise** is a beautiful garden, where the souls of the blessed will live in splendid palaces.

- **In European medieval legend**, the Land of Cockaigne was a paradise for idle, greedy people, where the rivers flowed wine and the buildings were made of cake.

- **Chinese Buddhists** believe in a heavenly paradise where souls appear as flowers before an enlightened female spirit called Dha-shi-zhi.

◀ The Celtic paradise of Tir Nan Og was a beautiful land without illness, old age or death.

Pharaohs and pyramids

- **The Ancient Egyptians** believed that people could enjoy life after death by preserving the body through mummification, putting food and personal possessions in their tomb and following elaborate funeral rites.

- **Part of mummification** involved removing the internal organs into pots called canopic jars.

- **Each mummy had a mask**, so every spirit could recognize its body.

- **People believed** that they would work in the afterlife, so models of their tools were buried with them. Pharaohs were buried with model servants called ushabtis, to work for them.

- **The Ancient Egyptians copied their funeral rites** from the funeral the god Horus gave to his father, Osiris. These were written in a work called *The Book of the Dead*.

- **One important funeral rite** was called the Opening of the Mouth ceremony.

- **Egyptian myth** says that the dead person's soul, or 'ka' was brought to an underworld Hall of Judgement.

▲ The Ancient Egyptians believed that the jackal-headed god, Anubis, brought the souls of the dead into an underworld courtroom to be judged good or bad.

- **First, a jackal-headed god called Anubis** weighed their heart against a feather of truth and justice. If the heart was heavier than the feather, it was devoured by a crocodile-headed god called Ammit.

- **If the heart was lighter than the feather**, the god Horus led the ka to be welcomed into the Underworld by the god Osiris.

- **People used to think** that the pharaohs enlisted slaves to build their pyramid tombs. Today, many historians think the Ancient Egyptians did this willingly, to please the gods and better their chances for life after death.

▼ Experts are baffled to this day as to how the Ancient Egyptians built their pyramids. Many theories have been tried out, but modern-day historians cannot explain satisfactorily how such vast quantities of stone could have been moved such huge distances and arranged with such incredible accuracy.

Realm of the dead

◄ Orpheus was told he was allowed to rescue his dead wife from the Underworld, as long as he didn't look at her on the journey back up to the world of the living. Tragically, he couldn't resist.

- **Greek myth says** that the poet Orpheus went down to the Underworld to try to bring back his wife, Eurydice.

- **According to Chinese myth**, a certain Buddhist monk once searched the Underworld for the soul of his mother. The gods kept him there as its ruler!

- **Greek myth says that when the god of the dead** kidnapped Persephone, the messenger god, Hermes went to the Underworld to persuade Hades to let her go.

- **A Thracian people** believed that the god Zalmoxis lived among humans. He once disappeared into the Underworld for three years, so he could teach people about the immortality of the soul.

- **In Norse myth**, the messenger god, Hermod, volunteered to go to the Underworld to try to bring the god Baldur back to life.

- **'Harrowing of Hell'** is a legend which says that Jesus journeyed into Hell and triumphed over evils there in the three days between his death and resurrection.

- **In the Roman epic** *The Aeneid*, the hero Aeneas travels to the Underworld where his father's ghost shows him a line of souls waiting to be born as his descendants.

- **The Mayan creator god**, Hunahpu, travelled into the Underworld with his brother, Ixbalangue. There they killed two demons, Hun Came and Vucub Caquix.

- **The Greek hero Odysseus** went into the Underworld to ask a dead seer, Tiresias, how he could find his way home from the Trojan Wars.

- **The Ancient Egyptians** believed that every night the sun god sailed through the Underworld, fighting demons and other evils.

Vampire mythology

- **Blood-drinking monsters** have featured in myths for thousands of years. Ancient Greeks believed in creatures called lamiae that ate children and drank bloosd. Stories from India from 3500 years ago tell of vampire-like creatures called Rakshasas.

- **Modern ideas about vampires** come from Eastern Europe: they are pale-skinned 'undead' who sleep in their coffins during the day and come out at night to drink blood and turn other people into vampires.

- **The word 'vampir'** is Slavic in origin.

- **Another word for vampires** is 'nosferatu'.

- **People believe** there are three ways to kill a vampire:
  (1) drive a wooden stake through the vampire's heart,
  (2) expose the vampire to sunlight,
  (3) set the vampire on fire.

◄ Garlic is traditionally thought to be a weapon against vampires. Legend says it is also a cure for warts!

- **Myths say you can ward off** vampires with crucifixes, holy water and garlic.

- **The most famous vampire is Count Dracula** who lived in a castle in Transylvania, Romania. The myth may have come from the real-life, blood-thirsty Vlad the Impaler, the Romanian tyrant, also known as Dracula.

- **Around 1560**, a noblewoman called Elizabeth Bathory killed over 600 girls in order to drink their blood. She believed this would keep her youthful.

- **The rare medical condition porphyria** could account for some vampire myths. It causes sensitivity to sunlight and garlic, and makes gums shrink, giving the incisor teeth the appearance of 'fangs'.

- **Vampire myths** have inspired many famous books, films and TV programmes, including: *Dracula* by Bram Stoker and *Buffy the Vampire Slayer*.

Doom and disappearance

- **Legend says** that a 'deathly' curse was written upon pharaoh Tutankhamun's tomb, discovered by Howard Carter in November 1922. No such curse was found.

- **The Bible story of the prophet Elijah** says that he didn't die, but drove up to heaven in a chariot of fire.

- **Bruce Lee**, martial artist and film star, fell into a coma in 1973 and died, aged 32. According to one myth, he was killed by an enemy in the martial arts world.

- **Russian tsar Nicholas II** and his family were executed in 1918 after the Russian Revolution. Legend says that one daughter, Anastasia, escaped.

- **The legend of Lord Lucan** tells how he vanished, never to be seen again, on 7 November 1974 – the same day that his children's nanny was found murdered at their home.

◀ *The Mary Celeste was a small trading vessel bound from New York for Genoa. Her crew mysteriously disappeared.*

- **The Egyptian queen Nefertiti**, wife of a rebel pharaoh, Akhenaten, tried to change traditional religious beliefs and made many enemies. No one knows how she died and her mummy has not been found.

- **A legend told by Catholics** in Northern Ireland said the *Titanic*, which sunk on 14 April 1912, was cursed because the shipbuilders gave her the number 3909 04, which looks like 'no pope' if read backwards.

- **Explorer Laurence Oates** became ill and committed suicide in 1912 on an Antarctic expedition led by Captain Scott. Legend says he walked out of his tent, saying: 'I am going out now. I may be some time.'

- **The legend of the *Mary Celeste*** tells of a ship found drifting in the Atlantic Ocean in December 1872. The entire crew had vanished without trace.

- **The Ring**, a modern film based on the ancient Japanese tradition of ghost legends, tells how anyone who watches a strange videotape meets a mysterious death seven days later.

Defeating death

- **Christian stories** say that Jesus could raise people from the dead.

- **Norse myth says** that when the god of light, Baldur, was killed, the goddess of death, Hela, said she would give him back his life if all living thing in the universe wept for him. All did except one – the evil god Loki.

- **Siberian people believed** that their holy men (or sharmans) became even more powerful after death.

- **The Khoi people of South Africa** tell a myth in which a man called Tsui'goab defeated Death in a wrestling match to save his village from perishing in a drought.

- **Greek myth says that the hero Heracles** once wrestled Death to win back the life of a woman called Alcestis.

- **A Hindu myth** tells how the Lord of Death had a child by a human woman without telling her who he was.

- **In Russian myth** Koschchei, a wizard, cheats death by keeping his soul inside an egg, inside a duck, inside a hare, inside an iron chest, under an oak tree, on an island in the middle of a wide ocean.

- **According to Greek myth** an elderly couple, Philemon and Baucis, were such good people that the gods granted them a wish to die together. The gods turned them into trees, which twined their branches around each other in an eternal embrace.

- **King Arthur's knights** were once challenged by a giant Green Knight to cut off his head. Sir Gawain bravely volunteered. However, the Green Knight just picked up his head and stuck it back on again!

- **The myth that cats have nine lives** tells of a witch's cat that found out how to turn himself into human form. Then he tried to get himself killed nine times to use up his cat's lives so as to remain human forever.

▶ *In the Arthurian myth of Sir Gawain, the character of the Green Knight has its roots in traditional beliefs about a 'green man of the woods' – the spirit of nature which dies and is reborn each year.*

Ghosts and ghouls

◄ The Legend of Sleepy Hollow *was made into a Hollywood movie in 1999, directed by Tim Burton and starring Johnny Depp and Christina Ricci.*

- **The Japanese** believe that after death a soul is angry. They carry out rituals over seven years to purify it into a peaceful spirit or it will return to as a ghost.

- **The Maya** believed that each person had a ghostly animal spirit called a nagual to accompany them.

- **In Eastern European legends**, Rusalki were souls of unbaptized babies or drowned young girls who turned into river spirits.

- **A house in Amityville**, New York, was haunted by terrifying happenings after a man called Ronald Defeo shot his family there on 13 November 1974. The legend became known as the Amityville Horror.

- **A duppy is a West Indian ghost** believed to appear if you throw coins and a glass of rum onto its grave.

- **People in Eastern European countries** believed in ghosts called Wila – the restless spirits of dead young women who had lived frivolous lives.

- *The Legend of Sleepy Hollow* tells of the terrifying ghost of a headless horseman. The American writer Washington Irving (1783–1832) wrote the story, based on a Dutch legend.

- **The Tower of London in England** is said to be haunted by many ghosts who were imprisoned. One is Anne Boleyn, beheaded wife of Henry VIII.

- **Drifting gaseous flames** can sometimes be seen at night over marshy land. These were thought to be the wandering ghosts of children – 'will o' the wisps'.

- **The Flying Dutchman** is a ghost ship which is said to lure real ships into danger around the Cape of Good Hope at the southern tip of Africa.

Spirit journeys

- **Many ancient tribal peoples** believed that their holy leaders, or 'shamans', could leave their bodies and journey through the spirit world.

- **Polynesian myth** tells that the dead walk down a path called Mahiki, through a seaside cave, to reach the world of spirits, Lua-o-Milu.

- **The Maya believed** that the road to the Underworld was steep and dangerous. It was covered with thorns and gushing torrents of water tried to sweep souls away into abysses on either side.

- **A story from the Book of Genesis** in the Bible tells that Jacob once saw angels going up and down a ladder between Earth and heaven.

► *This kachina, or spirit figure, was made by the Hopi people of North America. The Hopi honour the spirits of the Sun, winds, rain and maize plants.*

- **According to Classical myth**, Charon was the ferryman who sailed souls to the Underworld.

- **Plains Native Americans** believed that souls had to cross a bridge to the afterlife guarded by an Owl Woman. She flung off unidentified souls into an abyss below.

- **Muslim stories say that Al Sirat** is the bridge to heaven. It is narrower than a spider's thread and sharper than a sword. Wicked souls fall off it into hell.

- **Ancient Persian** stories say that the Chinvat bridge to heaven is guarded by an angel called Rashnu. He holds golden scales to weigh the souls of the dead.

- **The Ancient Egyptians** believed that souls travelled to the Underworld by boat, steered by Aken, the ferryman.

- **The Incas believed** that in order to reach paradise, Hanan Pacha, good souls had to cross a bridge woven from hairs.

Past and new lives

- **Voodoo myths in Africa and the Caribbean** tell of zombies – dead people who are brought back to life, but without minds or feelings.

- **Medieval Jewish legends** tell of rabbis who made golem – clay people who are brought to life by means of a charm to become zombie-like servants.

- **Hindu stories say that the god Vishnu** has appeared on Earth in nine incarnations to help humans. These nine forms are known as 'avatars'.

- **Hindus** believe that when a person dies, their soul moves on to a new life. If the person was good, their new life will be better. If the person was bad, they will be reincarnated into a harsh life of suffering.

- **According to Buddhist tradition**, a person who lives a selfish life is likely to be born again as a hungry ghost called a preta, whose greed can never be satisfied.

- **For the Maya**, the sea-snail was a symbol of resurrection after death.

◀ In modern myth, Frankenstein is a hideous zombie-like monster who is created and brought to life by a mad scientist.

- **Egyptian myth** says the goddess Isis resurrected the murdered god Osiris by searching for his scattered body and then restoring him to life by using the rites of embalment.

- **Heqt was the Egyptian goddess of resurrection**. She was pictured with the head of a frog.

- **Frankenstein was created** by a scientist from parts of dead human bodies and brought to life with the help of electricity. This myth developed from *Frankenstein*, the 1816 novel by Mary Shelley, in which Frankenstein was the name of the scientist, not the monster.

- **Advances** in genetic engineering mean scientists now, in theory, can create humans in the laboratory. The Frankenstein myth could become reality.

Visions of the end

- **Stories about the end of the world** are said to be eschatological myths. Tales about the creation of the world are called cosmogonical.

- **In the Bible**, Saint John predicts that four mighty horsemen representing war, famine, plague and death will appear at the end of the world.

- **The Fon tribe of Africa** believe the world is circled by a huge sea snake. One day, he will not be able to carry the weight and will sink to the bottom of the ocean.

- **The Aztecs believed that at the end of the world**, their god Quetzalcoatl would return to them. When the Spaniards invaded in 1519, the Aztecs believed that the Spanish leader was the returning Quetzalcoatl.

- **An Inca story** says that if mankind becomes too wicked, Viraccocha will weep a flood of tears that will sweep humans away.

- **Norse myth tells of Ragnarok**, which means 'the doom of the gods'. A huge battle will take place between the forces of evil and the forces of good – which evil will win. Then a new universe will be born.

- **Jewish mythology** tells of an angel called Israfel. He spends all eternity holding a trumpet to his lips, ready for God to tell him to announce the end of the world.

- **In Persian myth**, the end of time begins when a chained dragon, Azhi Dahaka, breaks free.

- **According to Islamic myth**, people have an angel who follows them and writes what they do – good and bad.

- **People** thought that humans would be destroyed by nuclear war. Now they think we will be wiped out by a deadly virus or a natural disaster.

▶ Islamic stories say that angels write down people's deeds, so God can judge them at the end of the world.

INDEX

Acknowledgements

The publishers would like to thank the following artists who contributed to this book:
Julie Banyard, C.M. Buzer (Luigi Galante Studio), Vanessa Card, Jim Channell,
Peter Dennis (Linda Rogers), Nicholas Forder, Chris Forsey, Terry Gabbey, Luigi Galante (Luigi Galante Studio), Alan Hancocks, Sally Holmes, Richard Hook, Rob Jakeway,
John James (Temple Rogers), Barry Jones, Roger Kent, Stuart Lafford, Priscilla Lamont, Kevin Maddison, M Mangeri (Luigi Galante Studio), Janos Marffy, Tracey Morgan,
Chris Odgers, Roger Payne, Rachel Phillips, Gill Platt, Terry Riley, Martin Sanders, Peter Sarson, Susan Scott, Caroline Sharpe, Rob Sheffield, Pam Smy, Roger Stewart,
Gwen Tourret, Peter Utton, Rudi Vizi, Steve Weston, Mike White (Temple Rogers), John Woodcock

The publishers would like to thank the following sources for the photographs used in this book:
Page 14 The Art Archive; 20 Universal/Dreamworks/Scott Free/Pictorial Press;
22 The Art Archive/Archaeological Museum Aleppo Syria/Dagli Orti;
28 New Line Productions/Pictorial Press; 33 RKO/Pictorial Press; 43 The Art Archive/Eileen Tweedy; 49 Historical Picture Archive/CORBIS; 61 Universal/Pictorial Press

All other pictures are from the Miles Kelly Archives
Corbis, Corel, digitalSTOCK, digitalvision, Dover, Hemera, ILN, PhotoAlto, PhotoDisc